Cambridge Elements ≡

Elements in the Philosophy of Mathematics
edited by
Penelope Rush
University of Tasmania
Stewart Shapiro
The Ohio State University

HUSSERL'S PHILOSOPHY OF MATHEMATICAL PRACTICE

Mirja Hartimo
University of Helsinki

T0372478

CAMBRIDGE
UNIVERSITY PRESS

CAMBRIDGE
UNIVERSITY PRESS

Shaftesbury Road, Cambridge CB2 8EA, United Kingdom

One Liberty Plaza, 20th Floor, New York, NY 10006, USA

477 Williamstown Road, Port Melbourne, VIC 3207, Australia

314–321, 3rd Floor, Plot 3, Splendor Forum, Jasola District Centre,
New Delhi – 110025, India

103 Penang Road, #05–06/07, Visioncrest Commercial, Singapore 238467

Cambridge University Press is part of Cambridge University Press & Assessment,
a department of the University of Cambridge.

We share the University's mission to contribute to society through the pursuit of
education, learning and research at the highest international levels of excellence.

www.cambridge.org
Information on this title: www.cambridge.org/9781009517072

DOI: 10.1017/9781009165709

First published 2024

A catalogue record for this publication is available from the British Library

ISBN 978-1-009-51707-2 Hardback
ISBN 978-1-009-16571-6 Paperback
ISSN 2399-2883 (online)
ISSN 2514-3808 (print)

Husserl's Philosophy of Mathematical Practice

Elements in the Philosophy of Mathematics

DOI: 10.1017/9781009165709
First published online: November 2024

Mirja Hartimo
University of Helsinki
Author for correspondence: Mirja Hartimo, mirjahartimo@gmail.com

Abstract: *Husserl's Philosophy of Mathematical Practice* explores the applicability of the phenomenological method to philosophy of mathematical practice. The first section elaborates on Husserl's own understanding of the method of radical sense-investigation (Besinnung), with which he thought the mathematics of his time should be approached. The second section shows how Husserl himself practiced it in tracking both constructive and platonistic features in mathematical practice. Finally, the third section situates Husserlian phenomenology within the contemporary philosophy of mathematical practice, where the examined styles are more diverse. Husserl's phenomenology is presented as a method, not a fixed doctrine, applicable to study and unify philosophy of mathematical practice and the metaphysics implied in it. In so doing, this Element develops Husserl's philosophy of mathematical practice as a species of Kantian critical philosophy and asks after the conditions of possibility of social and self-critical mathematical practices.

Keywords: philosophy of mathematical practice, Husserl, phenomenology, philosophy of mathematics, mathematical practice

ISBNs: 9781009517072 (HB), 9781009165716 (PB), 9781009165709 (OC)
ISSNs: 2399-2883 (online), 2514-3808 (print)

Contents

Introduction

During the first decades of the twenty-first century philosophy of mathematical practice was consolidated as a research tradition on its own. In this development, Ferreirós and Gray's *Architecture of Modern Mathematics: Essays in History and Philosophy* (2006) and Mancosu's *Philosophy of Mathematical Practice* (2008) as well as the founding of *Association for the Philosophy of Mathematical Practice* in 2009 were pivotal. Instead of representing their subject matter with general and normative theories, philosophers of mathematical practice call for seeing mathematics as a practice, as an outcome of individuals working in various kinds of institutional settings, with varying kinds of histories, with different kinds of goals, values, and styles of doing mathematics. The attention to actual practice has led to a plethora of detailed case studies that are used as the basis for the philosophical, historical, cognitive scientific, sociological, and so forth, studies about the nature of mathematical practice. A related shift can be detected in historiography of mathematics: there the focus on practice has led the historians of mathematics to emphasize diverse contingent factors that have influenced the conception and the dissemination of new ideas. This contrasts with the old pure "Whig" history that saw the development of mathematics as a linear progress toward the present situation (cf. Corry 2004, p. 4). In the analytic philosophy of mathematics, the shift resonates with the rise of naturalism and with the emphasis on the mathematics-first views as thematized by Stewart Shapiro and Penelope Maddy. The recent culmination of philosophy of mathematical practice is the publication of an encyclopedic *Handbook of the History and Philosophy of Mathematical Practice* (2024) that covers topics ranging from the metaphysics and ethics of mathematics to historical accounts of proofs, diagrams, and definitions, from studies of individual theories to the role of experiments in mathematical practice, from sociology, pedagogy, and semiotics of mathematical practices to the question of its connection to religion. The field is diverse and unified merely in its unprejudiced openness with which actual mathematics and its history are approached (for a particularly useful overview of the early development of the discipline, see Giardino 2017).

Speaking of all the sciences, but in a manner easily applicable to the present state of philosophy of mathematical practice, Husserl lamented that

> ... the list of special sciences has become so long that nobody is able any more to derive full advantage from all this wealth, to survey and enjoy all these treasures of cognition. The defect in our scientific situation ... concerns, not the collective unifying and appropriating of the sciences, but their *rootedness in principles* and their unification as springing from these roots. It

is a defect that would remain, even though an unheard-of mnemonics and a pedagogy guided thereby were to make possible for us an encyclopedic knowledge of what has at any particular time been ascertained with theoretical objectivity in all sciences. Science, in the form of special science, has become a sort of theoretical technique, which, like technique in the usual sense, depends on a "practical experience" accruing from many-sided and often-exercised practical activity itself – on what, in the realm of practice, is called "intuition", a knack, or a good practical eye – much more than on insight into the *ratio* of its accomplished production. (1969, p. 3, italic in the original)

Husserl calls for *rootedness in principles* with which rational unity should be brought to the plethora of scientific disciplines. This, perhaps outdatedly foundationalist sounding call should not be understood as a call for foundations in terms of the "foundationalist filter" (cf. Corfield 2003), or in a manner of intuitionism, logicism, and formalism, but for clarification of how the various, as such one-sided fragments of scientific knowledge relate to the common origin of cognition, namely subjectivity. This kind of reflection yields an overview of the sub-disciplines, their tasks, and relationships to each other and the subjectivity embedded in the lifeworld which, in Husserl's view, is needed for scientific self-responsibility as already Plato depicted.

This Element seeks to show how Edmund Husserl's writings can be used to bring some unity to the plethora of case studies, methods, and topics in philosophy of mathematical practice without at the same time lapsing into an a priori normative view of it, without reducing anything away from the richness of the discipline, or stifling the development of the examined phenomena. This is thanks to the largely descriptive, mathematics-first nature of Husserl's method. The claim is that Husserl's maxim "Back to the things themselves!" captures the common ethos of the phenomenologists and the philosophers of mathematical practice to return to a close study of the phenomena.[1]

This method is a combination of what Husserl called *"Besinnung'* of the mathematicians" enterprises and the transcendental analysis of the results of Besinnung. Besinnung is a methodological tool that Husserl developed in his later writings. Husserl, like the philosophers of mathematical practice, expanded his analyses to include the socio-historical context of the experiences and their objects. Accordingly, he started to view the sciences, mathematics, and logic explicitly as "formations [*Kulturgestalten*] produced indeed by the practice of the scientists and generations of scientists who have been building them"

---

[1] The phrase "Back to the things themselves!" derives from Husserl's Introduction to *Logical Investigations* (Husserl 1984, 2001a, §2). The things themselves are not Kantian things in themselves but the experienced phenomena. The phrase is supposed to remind the philosopher to study experiences, not to build theoretical or normative constructs.

(1974, p. 13, 1969, p. 9). He saw these practices and their development as teleological, that is, as goal-directed, and started to emphasize the scientists' (including the mathematicians') explicit or implicit goals, which sometimes are newly created but typically inherited from the previous generations. To find out what mathematics is for the mathematicians in these historical situations, Husserl argues, we need a "Besinnung [sense-investigation]." Sense-investigation aims at capturing the intentions of the mathematicians with a special emphasis on the epistemic goals and values that determine the practice in question. The method tries to capture the practitioner's point of view on their subject matter and as such it comes close to what for example Maddy advocates as the Second Philosopher's methodology (the differences are discussed in Section 3.2.2).

In addition to sense-investigation, the method calls for the extra-mathematical reflection on the transcendental conditions of the experiences. In *Formal and Transcendental Logic* (1929) Husserl calls such transcendental clarification, the "subjective theme" as opposed to the scientist's natural, objective theme (Husserl 1974, 1969, §§8–11). The subjective theme is the "anonymous" side of the experience to which we usually do not pay any attention at all. Here is Husserl's example from geometry:

> [T]he geometer, for example, will not think of exploring, besides geometrical shapes, geometrical thinking. It may be that shifts to the subjective focus are occasionally helpful or even necessary to what he truly has in view, namely the theory of his province; as in other far-seeing actions, so in theoretical actions the need may arise to deliberate reflectively and ask, "What method shall I try now? What premises can serve me?" (Husserl 1974, 1969, §9)

So, Husserl counts among the subjective theme a reflection about which axioms to accept and deliberation about which methods to use. The subjective direction of the inquiry investigates the tacit features of scientific thinking and its objects, and thus it provides a kind of "meta-perspective" on the objective theme. This "meta-perspective" is unified in being first-personal. In a Kantian manner the source of this unity is in the ego that constitutes everything given to it.

Phenomenology of mathematical practice thus brings a first-personal critical point of view to the naturalist "anything-goes" of the philosophy of mathematical practice. The phenomenologist's aim is to be true to the real, historically shaped social practices and to accommodate the findings of formal and empirical sciences. At the same time, the aim is to maintain the irreducible first-personal critical point of view to these practices and thereby to bring to them the awareness of who we are and what we are doing. The unity to the otherwise disperse findings of the philosophy of mathematical practice comes from

clarification and classification of the goals, concepts, and principles in various strands of mathematical practice, from relating them to various ways of
construction, and ultimately relating these to each other as well as to the
subjectivity.

This Element is organized into three sections. The first section explains
Husserl's method of approaching scientific practice as a combination of sense-
investigation (*Besinnung*) and transcendental clarification. The section also
addresses the metaphysical neutrality of this method, which is later needed to
detail the implied metaphysical picture. In the end this discussion will help us to
compare the phenomenological approach to Maddy's naturalism.

The second section focuses on a few of Husserl's results that are particularly
interesting from the point of view of the philosophy of mathematical practice,
namely the way he isolates the constructivist and the structuralist tendencies in
mathematics. It focuses on two main normative ideals or goals that Husserl
identified in mathematics. These can be seen as a top-down Euclidean and
a bottom-up, constructive, judgment-theoretical approach respectively. I will
discuss these goals as "formal" and "contentual" definiteness that in Husserl's
texts receive a variety of formulations. I will argue that Husserl analyzed them
as categoricity and constructivistic decidability, respectively. Husserl's attempts
thus confirm Ferreirós and Grey's (2006) characterization of the two mathematical styles, "postulationism" and "constructivism" around the turn of the
nineteenth century.

The second part of this section will then examine in detail what Husserl has to
say about the transcendental aspects of mathematical practice, that is, the kinds
of evidence intended in it as well as the assumed presuppositions, such as the
logical principles (e.g., *Modus ponens* and the law of the excluded middle). The
section will conclude with an account of what Husserl says about the constitution of abstract objects and how they are related to internal time-consciousness.

The third section then offers some reflections on what a Husserlian philosophy of mathematical practice could look like today. Given the richness of the
topic the section works more like an invitation for others to follow the suit.
Luckily, we do not need to start from scratch. Some existing approaches share
the spirit of natural Besinnung and can be taken as a starting point for phenomenology of mathematical practice (e.g., Maddy's work as discussed especially in
Section 3.2. Or take the model theoretical attempt at systematic classification of
theories after Shelah as discussed by Baldwin (2018)). Despite the much more
diversified practices, guided by more numerous and more subtly defined desired
properties, the inescapable transcendental aspect of these practices remains
largely the same as it was at Husserl's time. Mathematics is still human activity,
and its practice presupposes consciousness and its temporality. Thus, the

ultimate source of unity for all human enterprises is still in the ego that is the unifying pole of all constitution and everything constituted, whether given platonistically or constructively.

Whereas the earlier sections are based on close readings of Husserl's writings, with only occasional pointers to how to interpret them in today's context, the main aim of Section 3 is to reflect on their importance today. The section will further characterize the phenomenological philosophy of mathematics by comparing it to some other approaches. I will argue that phenomenology of mathematics should take the actual and real practice of mathematics at face value (because the method is metaphysically neutral). This distinguishes Husserl's view of mathematics from the classical foundational approaches. Whereas, for example, Frege devised his concept-script to give arithmetic a logical foundation and to show that the mathematical concepts, such as that of number, can be reduced to what can be constructed in logical concept-script, Husserl, while wanting to clarify the basic concepts of arithmetic, did not want to reduce mathematics to anything more primary but to describe it as it is. I have discussed Husserl vis-à-vis Frege several times before (Hartimo 2021a, 2021c, 2006), and others have done so as well (although with different and varying agendas; see, e.g., Føllesdal 1958; Cobb-Stevens 1990, and Hill and Rosado Haddock 2000), so I will not dwell on the issue of logicism on this occasion. I will not discuss Husserl's approach in comparison to Hilbert's project either (on this, see Hartimo 2017a, 2021a), nor do I discuss Gödel's theorems (for that, again, Hartimo 2021a and 2017b and the references therein).

Instead, I will explore three further themes in connection with the views developed here: the philosophy of mathematical practice, mathematical naturalism, social constructivism. Paolo Mancosu (2008) presents the philosophy of mathematical practice as growing out of two traditions, the first having its origins in Lakatos's work and then continued especially by Philip Kitcher, the second originating in Quine and today consisting of Penelope Maddy's naturalism. I will first briefly state how the Husserlian approach compares to the former tradition as discussed by Mancosu (2008). After this I will compare the phenomenological approach to Maddy's view. I will argue that the phenomenological approach differs from Maddy's Second Philosophy in two main ways: first, whereas Maddy's meta-perspective on mathematical practice is empirical, the phenomenologist engages in transcendental investigation of it. Second, whereas the phenomenologist wants to capture the practitioner's presupposed metaphysical views, Maddy's Second Philosopher does not respect the mathematician in philosophical matters and argues, somewhat reductionistically, that all that matters for mathematical practice is the practice itself.

This occasions a closer examination of Husserl's view of metaphysics. While his method is metaphysically neutral (and hence does not meddle with the practitioner's point of view), it has metaphysical implications in articulating the practitioner's largely implicit views. I will argue that the Husserlian view of metaphysics, especially as it is developed in his later "generative" period (i.e., when he includes socio-historical aspects in his analysis), amounts *to consti-tuted realism internal to a socially constructed historical tradition.* This aims to do justice to the practice of mathematics: while it is an uncontroversial fact that mathematical theories are socially constructed, nevertheless they are about abstract objects that the mathematicians typically view as transcendent, valid even before they were constructed.

This project leads to elaborating the way in which mathematical objects are related to time-consciousness. Husserl wants to make sense of all of mathematics as a historically conditioned social practice, given in a medley of levels and kinds of evidence. For Husserl, time-consciousness is a transcendental condition of the possibility of any experience. It is the subjective underpinning of all experiences, all givenness, and also of those objects that are actively constructed on a higher, intersubjective and intergenerational level.

Finally, as a terminological note, let me also point out that I use the term "evidence" to translate German *Evidenz.* The term refers to the seeing that something is so, that it is "being given," or "being self-given," *not* to the legal sense of the English term, that is, evidence for something or against someone, what in German would be *"Beweismittel."*[2]

1 "Back to the Things Themselves"

In her article "Phenomenology and Mathematical Practice," Mary Leng explained that "[t]he phenomenological philosopher of mathematics starts by taking a good look at mathematics, and only then asks, and tries to answer, philosophical questions about the discipline" (2002, p. 3).[3] Leng goes on to describe the phenomenological philosophy of mathematical practice helpfully and insightfully, except that she, somewhat surprisingly, traces the origins of such phenomenological philosophy of mathematics to Lakatos's *Proofs and Refutations.* Her reason for dismissing Husserl is that

---

[2] George Heffernan has discussed the notion and the problems of its translation usefully in an unpublished manuscript entitled "The Question concerning *Evidenz* in Husserl's *Erfahrung und Urteil* and *Formale und transzendentale Logik.*" In it, Heffernan points out that while *Evidenz* refers to "self-giving," phenomenology does not operate with "a given" naïvely, but that the phenomenology of evidence demythologizes "the myth of the given" by describing "the given" in terms of the taken, for there is no "giving" without a "taking." In other words, the given is *constituted,* as described earlier, and thus requires acts of consciousness to be had.

[3] This section elaborates on many issues discussed in Hartimo & Rytilä 2023.

Husserl advocates close consideration of the objects of mathematics, such as numbers, rather than the practices of mathematicians. A phenomenological study of mathematics which followed Husserl's lead would consider our idea of number, for example, and ask how that idea occurs. (Leng 2002, p. 5)

Instead, Leng proposes using the term "phenomenological philosophy of mathematics" to describe the practitioner's interest in "the point of view" belonging to mathematics (2002, p. 5). In this section, my aim is to argue that in his later texts, Husserl spells out a method with which to capture the point of view of the practicing mathematician.

Husserl's original focus was, indeed, the concept of number – in his *Philosophy of Arithmetic* (1891), Husserl described our commonsensical idea and origin of the number concept. But, thanks to the more general development in mathematics, Husserl gave up this restriction and in his *Prolegomena to Pure Logic* (1900),[4] Husserl writes:

> Only if one is ignorant of the modern science of mathematics, particularly of formal mathematics, and measures it by the standards of Euclid or Adam Riese, can one remain stuck in the common prejudice that the essence of mathematics lies in number and quantity. (Husserl 1975, 2001a, §71)

Husserl thought that formal mathematics is a study of structures, not of number or quantity. Already here Husserl tries to capture the practicing mathematicians' thoughts about their subject matter. In his view, the mathematicians aimed to disclose formal structures. He took the prevailing, structural view of mathematics as a norm guiding the practice of mathematics, even though he did not yet properly address the practice itself. For example, he envisioned a theory of theories, which he held Riemann, Cantor, Grassmann, Lie, and others had until then only provisionally worked out and which served as a more or less implicit *goal* of the nineteenth-century mathematical practice (Husserl 1975, 2001a, §70). In this sense, his approach was teleological already in *Logical Investigations*, and hence not static.[5]

With time, Husserl's investigations become more and more encompassing, and sometimes the new findings required revisions in his initial views.[6] By the

---

[4] The way in which Husserl's view responds to the developments in mathematics in the late 19th century is discussed, for example, in Hartimo 2010.
[5] I discuss this at length in Hartimo 2021a, esp. pp. 25–28. For a static view, see, for example, Ferreirós 2016, pp. 64–65.
[6] He explains the way he made progress and the consequent shift between the first edition of *Logical Investigations* (1901) and the *Ideas I* (1913) with the following words: "as the horizon of my research widened, and as I became better acquainted with the intentional 'modifications' so perplexingly built on one another, with the multiply interlacing structures of consciousness, there came a shift in many of the conceptions formed in my first penetration of the new territory" (2001a, p. 3). His progress to his later "generative" view of phenomenology is similarly a result of

1920s he started to explicitly discuss science as an intersubjective and intergenerational praxis, and to maintain that its historical development had to be
included in its faithful description. This realization also applied to mathematics.

During this time, Husserl developed further the phenomenological method
with which to approach mathematics in a noncircular manner. The starting point
for him was the division of labor proposed in *Prolegomena to the Logical
Investigations* (Husserl 1975, 2001a, §71). Accordingly, mathematicians should
focus on working out their problems and devise new theories freely, whereas the
task of philosophy is to understand the essence of mathematics. By "essence" in
this connection, Husserl meant "essence" in the sense that encompasses its *telos*
that it seeks to actualize, that is, its purpose. Thus, the phenomenologist's task is
to grasp what mathematics is and what it should be according to its own sense.
Husserl further pointed out that the philosophers should not meddle with the
mathematicians' work, suggesting that the *telos* of mathematics can be found in
the mathematicians' activities, not in a priori normative, philosophical claims
(Husserl 1975, 2001a, §71). This yields a view that mathematics should be
approached on its own, and philosophy about it should be descriptive and
metaphysically neutral (to be discussed in more detail soon). Furthermore, on
pain of infinite regress, philosophers' methods could not be formal, and to do
justice to the ideal structures studied in modern mathematics, the method could
not be psychological.[7]

1.1 Correlation and Phenomenological Reduction

The phenomenological method that Husserl developed beginning with *Logical
Investigations* and then more maturely in *Ideas I* aims to describe the things
themselves and their givenness. Husserl often characterizes phenomenology as
a study of the correlation between an experienced object and its manners of
givenness, or more generally, the world and the givenness of its sense to
subjectivity.[8] The correlation refers to the way in which what we think of the

---

painstaking analyses in which he takes more and more factors into account. Characteristic of his
progress is that he takes into consideration previously unnoticed features – it is not marked by any
radical turns or shifts between metaphysical views, such as realism to idealism.

[7] To be sure, Husserl's argument against psychologism in logic in *Prolegomena* takes the objectivity of mathematics and logic for granted and argues that unless normative logic is derived from
such an objective and theoretical attitude, it falls prey to psychologism, which in turn leads to
relativism and skepticism about knowledge.

[8] Husserl discusses the notion of correlation in several different senses, such as a correlation
between an act and an object. The notion of correlation that is referred to here is different; it is
a correlation between the objective world and its subjective achievements. Phenomenology is
essentially a study of correlation in the sense defined here, which, Husserl claims, occurred to him
when working on *Logical Investigations* in 1898 (Husserl 1970b, p. 166n). The term "sense" or
Sinn likewise acquires many technical uses in Husserl's writings. For a recent attempt to reconcile

objective world as necessarily "structured" by the subject insofar as they experience it as intelligible. The objective world is the world as conceived in the natural attitude; that is, it can be our immediate lifeworld. It can also be an extension of our lifeworld, such as the world(s) of, say, microbiology, or of mathematics. These different "worlds" branch and are nested in diverse ways.

The natural attitude is the non-philosophical, everyday life attitude, in which we are in our daily lives when we are not reflecting on it. It is the attitude in which the mathematician is when proving something and focused on solving a certain problem. But, when one starts to deliberate what axioms one should have or what methods of proof one should use, one already starts to move to the "subjective" transcendental phenomenological attitude. This attitude seeks to clarify the natural attitude and the world given in it. In the case of mathematics, it is reflection on mathematical activity, starting with questions such as, say, which earlier results to use and what is the overall point of the activity.

To facilitate the move to the required reflective stance, Husserl devised the dramatic-sounding methodological moves, namely the *phenomenological epoché* and the *phenomenological reduction(s)* in *Ideas I* (Husserl 1976a, 2014, §§31–33). Their purpose is to bracket the everyday trust in the world so that the philosopher could focus on its constitution without the interference of the natural attitude interests. So, instead of thinking of how one is to prove something, the occupation with the proof is bracketed, so that one can move into the meta-perspective to reflect on the practice in question. The resulting stance is supposed to be "pure," precisely in this sense, that is, that it is unhindered by the natural attitude concerns. Hence, the transcendental consciousness is not empty; it contains everything we were aware of in the natural attitude, but now considered as the object of reflection. In this new attitude, we are able to examine how the natural attitude and the objects in it are constituted, that is, related to the subjectivity. Thus, the reduction aims to reveal the ideal structures with which we "clothe" the world and thereby see it as intelligible and meaningful. It purports to help us see how the mind is active even in a mere passive perception of an object. It reveals that we do not just passively receive sense-data, but we see the object, say, a cup of coffee, as three-dimensional, with a backside, and as a familiar object of a certain known type, and so forth – all these are kinds of "structures" with which we constitute the object as it appears to us. To be sure, for Husserl, the object appears incompletely with unseen adumbrations, but nevertheless as "it itself." There is no separate world of things themselves, but the natural world around us provides the subject matter

different kinds of interpretations, see Hirvonen 2022. In this passage I speak of "sense" in a vague and general manner as synonymous with "intelligibility."

for transcendental reflection. In this way the transcendental attitude is intimately connected to the natural attitude and the world given in it. Transcendental clarification without the underlying natural experiences that are reflected upon does not make any sense.

1.2 Metaphysical Neutrality and Critical Metaphysics

In *Logical Investigations*, Husserl characterizes phenomenology as free from metaphysical, scientific, and psychological presuppositions (1984, p. 28, 2001a, p. 179), and for this reason it is thought to be a "metaphysically neutral" method. David Carr has argued that, in this sense, Husserl's enterprise resembles Kant's in being an inquiry into the possibility of metaphysics, mathematics, and science. It does not add to their claims, nor replace them with new claims, but it inquires into how they are possible. Similarly, Husserl's transcendental phenomenology "does not consist of knowledge claims about the world, whether scientific or metaphysical. By 'bracketing' these claims, as we have seen, he turns his attention from the world and its objects to the experiences in which they are given. Like Kant, he emphasizes the 'how' question: the '"how" of manners of givenness'" (Carr 1999, p. 101).

Dan Zahavi has voiced a critique that Carr's and also Steven Crowell's (2001) interpretations lead to a "semantical interpretation" of Husserl's phenomenology which makes it into an analysis of meaning that is not concerned with reality (2002, pp. 110–111, 2017, pp. 63–64, 101). Zahavi argues further that metaphysical neutrality would make transcendental phenomenology compatible with a variety of metaphysical views, such as objectivism, eliminativism, or subjective idealism (2017, p. 101). This is, however, not what David Carr means by metaphysical neutrality. For him, the phenomenological method reflects upon the natural attitude itself, not upon philosophical views such as objectivism, eliminativism, or subjective idealism. According to Carr,

> [phenomenology] takes the natural attitude not as a premise for inferring the existence or nature of what exists outside the natural attitude. Instead, it keeps its focus on the natural attitude and asks after the conditions of its possibility. In a sense, the natural attitude remains the constant subject matter, the sole text, as it were, of all of phenomenology's investigations. (2022, p. 12)

And a few lines later, he adds: "the primary purpose of phenomenology, as we have seen, is to reflect upon and understand the natural attitude itself: its structures, its activities, in other words, its essence, including that of all the sciences that are built upon it or within it" (2022, p. 12). In Carr's view, transcendental phenomenology cannot be connected to whatever metaphysical views Zahavi seems to suggest a metaphysically neutral approach should be able to do. The views like objectivism, eliminativism, or subjective idealism would be metaphysical presuppositions, and Carr explicitly holds that phenomenology does not presuppose any metaphysical views (2022, p. 14).

It thus seems Zahavi exaggerates the way in which Carr thinks phenomenology is metaphysically neutral. But Carr also holds that phenomenology has no metaphysical implications either; that is, its investigations provide no support for realism, idealism, or skepticism (2022, p. 14). This is precisely where Zahavi disagrees: he argues that phenomenology cannot be metaphysically neutral because it has metaphysical implications. He also makes it clear that the dispute is not about the meaning of the term "metaphysics": after having displayed different kinds of views about what "metaphysics" means, he stipulates that he will "exclusively understand metaphysics as pertaining to the realism-idealism issue, i.e., to the issue of whether reality is mind-independent or not" (2017, p. 65).

The view advocated here agrees (and disagrees) with both parties of this dispute in holding that the transcendental phenomenological *method* is metaphysically neutral but also that it has metaphysical implications. This is because the transcendental phenomenological method is necessarily dependent on the subject's natural attitude – as Carr emphasizes – and the implicit "metaphysics" embedded in it. The metaphysical views implicit in the natural attitude are not theoretical, philosophers' views on metaphysics. Husserl thinks that we, human beings, hold all kinds of "natural" metaphysical commitments in our everyday lives. The phenomenological method, because of its metaphysical neutrality, does not aim at stripping these metaphysical commitments away from us. On the contrary, the phenomenological method seeks to clarify what exactly they are. They do not amount to naïve idealism or realism; these would be philosophical positions and hence by definition not something held in the natural attitude. Instead, the phenomenologist wants to clarify, for example, the mode of givenness of the objects and the underlying "thesis," that is, our natural reliance and belief that the world exists. Furthermore, in their practices, the mathematicians are committed to abstract entities in various ways. All this amounts to a metaphysics that is implicit in the natural attitude, to be revealed by the metaphysically neutral phenomenological method. Thus, Husserl's approach resembles that of Kant's in his rejection of naïve metaphysics but so that it makes room for critical metaphysics. This kind of understanding agrees with Husserl's claim in *Cartesian Meditations* that "phenomenology indeed excludes every naïve metaphysics that operates with absurd things in themselves, but does not exclude metaphysics as such" (1973a, 1999, §64).

Thus the metaphysical neutrality of transcendental phenomenology is here understood to mean that the method does not add anything to or take anything away from its object.[9] The everyday reality is described as it appears to be and no postulation of Kantian things-in-themselves should take place. Any explanatory metaphysical postulation or reduction is excluded from this description.

Even though the *method* itself is metaphysically neutral, the use of the method has metaphysical implications. This is because of the intimate connection between the natural attitude and the transcendental phenomenological attitude. Human beings have in their natural attitude a "natural" metaphysics (as opposed to *philosophical* metaphysics). This natural metaphysics is made explicit by the transcendental phenomenological attitude. The phenomenological method is metaphysically neutral in not being reductive about such implicit metaphysical claims. It is also metaphysically neutral in not reifying the implicit natural metaphysics into anything more than what it is.

The metaphysical *implications* are both negative and positive. The negative implications exclude certain (philosophical) metaphysical views. For example, the metaphysical neutrality of the method conflicts with certain theoretical postulations, such as naïve idealism or realism. Or, to take an example from the philosophy of mathematics, metaphysical neutrality excludes those positions that do not start with an examination of mathematics as it is, but approach mathematics with a theory first. Hence, the approach rules out intuitionist philosophical revisionism,[10] logicism, scientific naturalism, fictionalism, and so forth. The positive implications amount to making explicit the implicit metaphysics of the natural attitude.

Perhaps a comparison to Carnap can help in driving this point home: In his "Empiricism, Semantics, and Ontology," Carnap divides the questions concerning the existence or reality of entities into two kinds. Either they are internal or else external to the framework in which they are spoken about. Think of Carnap's frameworks as linguistic version of Husserl's intensional worlds of the natural attitude. In other words, the world is what one is committed to exist in each framework. The negative implications of the phenomenological method exclude external questions about the existence of abstract entities. External questions, as we are told by Carnap, are the questions that are raised neither

---

[9] This understanding of metaphysical neutrality is also captured by Husserl's "principle of all principles" in *Ideas I*, which declares that *"whatever presents itself to us in 'Intuition' in an originary way* (so to speak, in its actuality in person) *is to be taken simply as what it affords itself as,* but *only within the limitations in which it affords itself there"* (Husserl 1976a, 2014, §24, italic in the original). Another passage can be found in §22 of *Ideas I*: "In truth, everyone sees 'ideas,' 'essences,' and sees them, so to speak, all the time; everyone operates with ideas and essences in thinking – only from their epistemological 'standpoint' do they interpret those judgments away" (1976a, 2014, p. 48/40). The phenomenologist aims at capturing what "in truth" everyone assumes in their practices, prior to any theoretical views about it.

[10] Intuitionism is excluded in the sense of a philosophy-first, strongly revisionist approach. The practice of constructive mathematics is not excluded but taken at face value.

by the man in the street nor by scientists, but only by philosophers (1950, p. 22). David Carr seems to view metaphysical questions solely as external questions, thinking that phenomenology only addresses internal questions. The positive metaphysical implications of the phenomenological method relate to internal questions, which Carr probably does not see as counting as proper metaphysics any longer. Whereas for Carnap answers to these questions "may be found either by purely logical methods or by empirical methods," for Husserl the answers are given by the phenomenological method, that is, by describing the natural attitude and clarifying it transcendentally. The method is metaphysically neutral analogously to what Carnap's "purely logical methods or by empirical methods" purport to be. The result is an ontology somewhat along the lines of Amie Thomasson's easy ontology (cf. Thomasson 2014). It is also a kind of metaphysics in the sense described earlier, since it reveals a "natural" attitude toward idealism and realism and, for example, explains how the natural attitude is characterized by a fundamental "thesis," thanks to which we do not in the natural attitude doubt the existence of the world. This approach has the consequence of rendering metaphysics, understood as asking questions of idealism and realism, to be about our world.

Since the method aims to describe the mode of being of the objects that are initially encountered in the natural attitude, it describes the natural, that is, the unreflected and non-philosophized metaphysical beliefs, such as commitments to abstract objects. These are found out by studying the intentions of mathematicians in their practices, and they amount to commitments to structuralist, platonist, or constructivist elements, as we will see in the next section. To capture such implicit metaphysical beliefs, Husserl gives detailed descriptions of our natural attitude, which includes the common-sense beliefs as well as those of the theoretical attitudes of various disciplines. These descriptions yield descriptions of various regional material and formal ontologies (Husserl 1976a, 2014, §9; Hartimo & Rytilä 2023).

The metaphysical neutrality of the phenomenological method has a decisive role for what kind of philosophy of mathematics the phenomenological method yields. As we will see in Section 3, it makes the phenomenological point of view "mathematics-first" (like Maddy's Second Philosophy), and thanks to it, phenomenology seeks to make explicit the implicit metaphysics found in the mathematicians' intentions (contra Maddy, who thinks that for the practice of mathematics it does not make any difference whether the practitioner is a thin arealist or thin realist; I will get back to this in more detail in Section 3). I will argue that thanks to its metaphysical neutrality, the phenomenological philosophy of mathematics ought to be developed in a pluralistic spirit, without taking "sides" about how to develop the field.

1.3 Radical *Besinnung* in *Formal and Transcendental Logic*

Husserl's description of the phenomenological method as explained earlier does not yet fully meet Leng's criticism cited at the beginning of this section since it examines an object and its constitution without taking into account the full nexus of mathematical praxis. This aspect will be taken care of in Husserl's move from a "genetic" to the so-called "generative" phenomenology in the 1920s to also encompass the intergenerational and intersubjective aspects of experiences. In *Formal and Transcendental Logic* (1929), a book that he later held as his most mature publication, Husserl examines science (including mathematics) as a cultural formation produced "by the practice of the scientists and generations of scientists who have been building them" (1974, p. 13, 1969, p. 9), thus adopting a yet more encompassing point of view to his subject-matter. To understand this practice, he writes, philosophers have to enter into *a community of empathy* with the scientists:[11]

> As so produced, they [sciences] have a final sense, toward which the scientists have been continually striving, at which they have been continually aiming. Standing in, or entering, a community of empathy with the scientists [*Einfühlungsgemeinschaft*], we can follow and understand – and carry on "sense-investigation". [*Besinnung*]. (Husserl 1974, p. 13, 1969, p. 9)

The scientists' practice is determined by final senses, that is, the goals of the discipline in question that have guided the scientists for generations. Husserl thus wants to examine ideas in their historical context of purposive human action. He defines his method as "sense-investigation" [*Besinnung*] that aims to make explicit scientists' otherwise typically only vague goals:

> *Sense-investigation* [*Besinnung*] signifies nothing but the attempt actually to produce the sense "itself," which, in the mere meaning, is a meant, a presupposed, sense; or equivalently, it is the attempt to convert the "inten-tive sense" [*intendierenden Sinn*] . . ., the sense "vaguely floating before us" in our unclear aiming, into the fulfilled, the clear, sense, and thus to procure for it the evidence of its clear possibility. (Husserl 1974, p. 13, 1969, p. 9, italic in the original)

When applied to mathematics, this method aims at explicating the sometimes unclear point of mathematicians' practice. In writing this passage, Husserl may have thought of, for example, Hilbert, and the question of whether the point of his proof theory is to provide mathematics consistency, certainty, or truth. With

---

[11] Hence, Moon 2023 calls the Husserlian approach "empathy-first" approach. To be sure, the notion of "empathy" is extremely ambiguous. For Husserl, it does not mean experiencing or sharing others' emotions, but "seeing" what others' emotions are, and in *Besinnung*, understanding them in terms of what they are trying to do.

this method Husserl aims at procuring a practitioner's point of view by also taking into account the history of the discipline from its inception by the Greeks and thus a *"definitive clarification of the sense of purely formal mathematics . . .*, *according to the prevailing intention of mathematicians*: its sense, namely, as a *pure analytics of non-contradiction*, in which the concept of truth remains outside the theme" (1974, pp. 15–16, 1969, p. 11, italic in the original). In other words, he wants to account for pure mathematics and its genealogy. Note that he claimed to capture what mathematics is according to *the prevailing intention of its practitioners in the 1920s*, and as one of his main results that it is pure as opposed to applied mathematics. Thus, Husserl finally manages to explicate the method to carry out the philosophers' task as he envisioned it already in his division of labor of the *Prolegomena*.

As before, transcendental "meta-perspective" is also needed. In the first part of *Formal and Transcendental Logic*, Husserl engages in natural sense-investigation of logic and mathematics, by examining their historical developments as well as the "living intentions" of the mathematicians of his time. In the second part, Husserl adds the transcendental dimension to this investigation. Husserl characterizes transcendental clarification as follows:

> In naive intending and doing, the aiming can shift, as it can in a naive repetition of that activity and in any other going back to something previously striven for and attained. [. . .] Turning reflectively from the only themes given straightforwardly (which may become importantly shifted) to the activity constituting them with its aiming and fulfilment – the activity that is hidden (or, as we may also say, "anonymous") throughout the naive doing and only now becomes a theme in its own right – we examine that activity after the fact. That is to say, we examine the evidence awakened by our reflection, we ask it [the evidence] what it was aiming at and what it acquired; and, in the evidence belonging to a higher level, we identify and fix, or we trace, the possible variations owing to vacillations of theme that had previously gone unnoticed, and distinguish the corresponding aimings and actualizations. (Husserl 1974, 1969, §69)

In this quotation, Husserl first explains the natural, "naïve" attitude, such as the one that one is in when proving a theorem. After this he explains that the transcendental phenomenological clarification is "turning around" to reflect on this straightforward natural practice, and in particular examining what kind of evidence it was aiming at. This reflection is what Husserl means by "transcendental"; instead of naïve attitude, the reflection is carried out in the transcendental phenomenological attitude, and it aims to spell out the transcendental presuppositions of mathematical practice. Such transcendental reflection offers a kind of "meta-perspective" to the natural approach. However, it does not imply a semantic ascent and a consequent attempt at building a metatheory about the activity from a third-person point of view. Instead, it means sorting out and making explicit its transcendental conditions by reflecting on the presuppositions of the experiences within the experiences. The reflection is thus *transcendental* in terms deriving from Kant. It is *not transcendent*, that is, theorizing of what is beyond our experience, and it does not involve any mysterious or religious aspects either.[12]

The purpose of such clarification is to point out possible confusions and shiftings in the studied activity. Thus, the transcendental clarification has a critical aim so that " . . . that such evidence – evidence of every sort – should be reflectively considered, reshaped, analyzed, purified, and improved; and that afterwards it can be, and ought to be, taken as an exemplary pattern, a norm" (Husserl 1974, 1969, §69).

This criticism results in a "concomitant fixing of terminology," and appropriating the revised concepts so that they will persist "as acquisitions in the realm of habit" (Husserl 1974, 1969, §70b), in other words, it results in a kind of conceptual re-engineering. The transcendental clarification seeks to show the origin of conceptual confusions so that the philosopher can give guidance for fixing the concepts. The transcendental phenomenological clarification will help evaluate which account of mathematical practice is genuine [*echt*], that is, carried out with clarified and revised, if needed, concepts, principles, and theories, and so that it fulfills its theoretical goals that are likewise clarified. The ultimate aim is to give suggestions for revising scientific practices and the norms guiding them and to "give the sciences fundamental guidance thereby and to make possible for them genuineness in shaping their methods and in rendering an account of every step" (Husserl 1974, p. 7, 1969, p. 3). The philosopher's task is to make sure the rational practices in fact take place *rationally*, instead of proceeding "blindly" out of reliance on arbitrary techniques.

---

[12] In *The Crisis*, Husserl explains that he uses "the word 'transcendental' *in the broadest sense* for the original motif, . . . the motif of inquiring back into the ultimate source of all the formations of knowledge, the motif of the knower's reflecting upon himself and his knowing life in which all the scientific structures that are valid for him occur purposefully, are stored up as acquisitions, and have become and continue to become freely available" (Husserl 1976b, 1970b, §26, italic in the original). Husserl then criticizes Kant for not properly engaging in transcendental philosophy because Kant approaches the conditions of experience with a "mythically, constructively inferring method" instead of "a thoroughly intuitively disclosing method" (Husserl 1976b, 1970b, §30). Husserl's target here is, for example, Kant's derivation of the pure concepts of understanding from the table of judgments in B deduction, which is not an analysis of direct experience but a "theoretical" argument. The idea of transcendental *argument* does not make sense to Husserl. Husserl then describes the transcendental "aspect" of human life as another "dimension" found in the natural, normal human life, somewhat like the third dimension for the two-dimensional creatures, "the plane-beings." Husserl credits Helmholtz for the image of them, popularized by Edwin Abbott Abbott in a romantic novella *Flatland, a Romance of Many Dimensions* (1884) (Husserl 1976b, 1970b, §32).

All this amounts to explicating the "tacit dimension" of mathematicians' work. It aims to make explicit the kinds of evidence aimed at, but also the tacit presuppositions assumed in the research (such as the logical principles), and ultimately also the givenness of the ideal objects, the mode of being of the objects of mathematics as the mathematicians find them in their practices.

Ultimately, transcendental phenomenology takes Husserl to the problems of transcendental subjectivity to which all sciences are related (Husserl 1974, 1969, §103). It thus shows how mathematics is connected to the more general experiences and to the problems of how, for example, intersubjective embodied experience in general is constituted, and how our consciousness has a certain time-structure. Husserl's posthumously published work *Erfahrung und Urteil* traces the origin of logic (and mathematics) to the ego's striving for certainty and consistency. The former finds its origin in prepredicative experiences of receptivity (ultimate substrates) and the latter in the striving for harmony [*Einstimmigkeit*], so that everything that exists for the unified ego is organized in a single world (e.g., Husserl 1985, §§12 and §71).

In the interest of understanding mathematical practice, I will here stay within the problems specific to the formal theories, and hence of specific interest for the philosophy of mathematical practice. I will thus focus on Husserl's natural straightforward account of mathematical practice, for which the transcendental clarification provides an extra-mathematical analysis. In short, the task of transcendental clarification of mathematics is to explore all the kinds of evidence in which mathematical formations are given. It is critical reflection of what has been carried out in formal sciences, and its aim is to spot the possible conceptual confusions and shiftings and to make us aware of our idealizing presuppositions. Ultimately the transcendental presuppositions of experience are traced to, for example, intersubjectivity of the experiences and the temporal structure of consciousness. It is not clear to what extent the phenomenologist of mathematical practice needs to follow Husserl there.

So, to recap, Husserl's phenomenological method (with which he examines formal sciences) is a combination of methods: sense-investigation and transcendental clarification. While the method has critical aspects in aiming at revision of confused concepts and principles, making sure that they are applied in their proper scopes, and seeking to clarify the kinds of evidence, and so forth, it does not evaluate the experiences with a pregiven external conception of what it should be like. It suggests revisions on the basis of the mathematicians' explicated and clarified intentions "internal" to the practice. This reflection is never finished: there is no ideal state or mechanism that could conclusively settle the correctness of our thought.

2 Husserl's Phenomenology of Mathematical Practice

This section aims to show how Husserl's views about mathematics are derived from the practice of mathematics around the turn of the twentieth century. They are results of sense-investigation and they are either "formal" or else transcendental following the way in which Husserl's *Formal and Transcendental Logic* is structured. To be sure, "formal" means here something that is not "transcendental"; hence, it designates a rather loose sense of the term "formal," namely the natural sense used when referring to the formal sciences in general (mathematics, mathematical physics, or logic). Husserl's discussion of what he views as formal logic aims at explicating the essence of the formal sciences and, in particular, what the mathematicians' and logicians' implicit goals in developing it are. This relates his view of formal sciences to structuralism. Husserl thinks the mathematicians' one aim is to describe formal structures. Note that formal *logic* is not logic in the sense of a study of valid inferences, but it includes all of mathematics together with a theory of judgments within which the theories of mathematics are constructed. Husserl's discussion of the latter explicates the constructivist style of doing mathematics.

The transcendental part of the book, in turn, provides the former part of the book with the meta-perspective of the kind explained in the previous section. Husserl's transcendental clarification is about the givenness of exact sciences to the subject, that is, what kinds of evidence the mathematicians are seeking to acquire in their practices. The transcendental investigation also reveals all kinds of presuppositions held by the mathematicians and logicians (such as reiteration and the logical principles). Ultimately it shows how the sciences are related to the scientists' everyday world and perception or memory of (middle-sized) objects in it. In this sense, Husserl's transcendental logic has the same function as Kant's transcendental logic has in Kant's system.[13] However, the primary sense of the term "transcendental logic" for Husserl refers to an examination of the formal sciences from the transcendental point of view, that is, engaging in a reflection on the formal sciences from a transcendental meta-perspective.[14]

The section is divided into two parts where the first discusses the results of the formal part of the book and the second those found in the transcendental part of

---

[13] According to Kant, transcendental logic is a science by means of which we think of objects completely *a priori*: "Such a science, which would determine the origin, the domain, and the objective validity of such cognitions, would have to be called transcendental logic, since it has to do merely with the laws of the understanding and reason, but solely insofar as they are related to objects a priori and not, as in the case of general logic, to empirical as well as pure cognitions of reason without distinction" (A57/B81-82).

[14] Husserl writes of Kant's view of transcendental logic that it "is something entirely different from that (transcendental-phenomenological) inquiry concerning the subjective which we have in mind" (1974, 1969, §100).

it. As explained in the previous section, these results are carried out in two attitudes that are interdependent; they inform each other. Hence, many transcendental observations are discussed already in connection with the formal results, and many times, it seems, the transcendental clarification precedes the formal results. For example, as one of the main outcomes of his transcendental clarification, Husserl mentions the distinction between two kinds of evidence, clarity [*Klarheit*] and distinctness [*Deutlichkeit*]. Distinctness is a kind of evidence that relates to coherence – it is acquired from non-contradictory, meaningful judgments and consistent theories. It is gained from these judgments or theories alone, hence the concept of truth that in his view requires adequation with the states of affairs is excluded from it. It is a kind of evidence one may obtain by looking at the structure of the judgment or a theory alone, that the theory or judgment forms a harmonious unity.[15] The goal of truth, in turn, is given in the evidence of clarity [*Klarheit*], which is obtained when perceiving objects in the world. These kinds of evidence may shift; hence, transcendental clarification is needed to keep them separate and fixed. This distinction, Husserl claims, suggested to him the major distinction cutting across the formal sciences, namely that between pure and applied mathematics, that is, the logic of truth (1974, 1969, p. 12). The logic of truth is to him about the formal structures that obtain in the (suitably idealized) world. Thus, while the history of how mathematics became pure, and how pure mathematics is distinguished from, say, physical geometry, is complex (cf. Maddy 2008), Husserl's analysis of it is that the distinction between the two is ultimately a matter of the kind of evidence sought in them, and the distinction itself can be clarified by means of transcendental analysis. Thus, something belonging to the transcendental second part of the book guides the distinction already made in the formal first part of the book, thus witnessing the interdependence of the formal and the transcendental investigation.

In what follows, I will not even try to give a full picture of Husserl's view of formal theories (for this, see Bachelard 1968 and Hartimo 2021a). Instead, I will focus on what I find to be the most interesting themes in it from the perspective of the philosophy of mathematical practice. Indeed, I will focus on Husserl's

---

[15] In the *Lectures on First Philosophy*, Husserl explains, for example, that the "core" of a logic of non-contradiction is "constituted by rational theories that perpetuated themselves down through the millennia, however much logic in other respects may have undergone modifications. The theories were limited to the formal conditions of possibility governing the consistent fixing of judgments that have already been carried out, a fixing which is accomplished solely according to the analytic sense of these judgments and prior to any questions regarding their factual truth or possibility" (Husserl 2019, p. 20). We will return to a more detailed view of distinctness, but it should be noted that the consistency involved in it is not merely syntactic non-contradictoriness but also involves semantic elements.

concept of definite manifold, with which he claims to have attempted to give the Euclidean ideal a concrete formulation (1974, 1969, §31). Husserl discussed this concept in the most detail in his Double Lecture held at the Göttingen Mathematical Society in 1901, but it is mentioned in one way or another in all of Husserl's published works. I will also discuss Husserl's view of it in his *Logic and General Theory of Science*, the lecture course given by Husserl at the universities of Göttingen and Freiburg four times between 1910 and 1918. As we will soon see, definiteness bifurcates into formal and contentual definiteness, which I will analyze as categoricity and constructive decidability respectively. Husserl does not require that every theory should be categorical and further, he also suggests different kinds of views of constructivity, which suggests that formal and contentual definiteness should be viewed as *ideals*. For the most of his life, Husserl seemed to think that formal and contentual definiteness coincide, which was shown not to be possible in the 1930s. However, if viewed individually, these two goals are still relevant in clarifying the structuralist, on one hand, and the constructivist, on the other, elements in contemporary mathematics.

Having discussed Husserl's view of definiteness in the first part of this section, the second focuses on the transcendental results. As already mentioned, these include an account of various kinds of evidence. In addition to distinctness that accrues from non-contradictoriness and clarity that relates to truth, Husserl's logic is also governed by evidence related to grammatically correct judgments. These kinds of evidence are ultimately considered to be norms guiding exact sciences. In other words, in these sciences theories should be expressed in grammatically correct statements, they should be coherent and applicable to the world. Husserl's transcendental analyses imply a possibility of finding any number of further kinds of evidence corresponding to different kinds of (epistemic) values.

In addition to purifying and clarifying different kinds of evidence, the transcendental clarification reveals a number of idealizing presuppositions held in scientific inquiry, such as a presupposition of an ideal identity of judgments. Thanks to this, the concepts and the judgments remain the same independently of who utters them and they can also be recollected and reactivated later in time (1974, 1969, §73); reiteration (§74); the logical principles such as the law of contradiction and the law of the excluded middle (§§75–78); *modus ponens* (§78), and the fundamental presupposition that every judgment can be decided (§79). The role of logical principles as well as how Husserl thinks the abstract objects are given to the mathematicians will be discussed in more detail. The latter implies a question of whether the object in question is given as transcendent or not. As we will see, the givenness of the abstract objects includes what Husserl calls their mode of being. Hence, this consideration gives an analysis of how the mathematicians constitute the abstract objects (i.e., that they are conceived as transcendent and omnitemporal, etc.).

2.1 Formal and Contentual Definiteness as the Goals of Mathematical Practice

In *Formal and Transcendental Logic* (1929) Husserl discusses the historical development of formal sciences by identifying in it two separate strains: the development of logic as a theory of judgments (formal apophansis) since Aristotle and the development of mathematics into a formal science of anything-whatever, that is, into a formal ontology. Husserl gives the developments intentional explications in terms of the goals or ideals that define these strains. The development of the theory of judgments is guided by three kinds of evidence, grammaticality, distinctness, and truth. Mathematicians in turn were guided by the Euclidean ideal. Husserl holds that he "attempted to give [Euclidean ideal] concrete formulation in the *concept of the definite manifold* [Begriff der definiten Mannigfaltigkeit]" (1969, §31, italic in the original). Husserl eventually claims that these two strains are ultimately inseparable, because "all the forms of objects, all the derivative formations of anything-whatever, do make their appearance in formal apophantics itself" (1969, §25), that is, all acts in mathematics are in the end acts of judgment (Husserl's view of judgment comprises *all* theoretical objectivating acts in mathematics such as, collecting, counting, ordering, and combining (1974, 1969, §39)).

This takes us to the issue of definiteness [Begriff der definiten Mannigfaltigkeit]. It is explicitly identified as the goal of formal mathematicians. But Husserl's discussion of definiteness is ambiguous. For example, in his *Formal and Transcendental Logic* in 1929, Husserl compares definiteness to what Hilbert had in mind when he added his "axiom of completeness" to his axiomatizations of geometry and arithmetic around the turn of the century. Husserl writes:

> Throughout the present exposition I have used the expression "complete system of axioms", which was not mine originally but derives from Hilbert. Without being guided by the philosophico-logical considerations that determined my studies, Hilbert arrived at his concept of completeness (naturally quite independently of my still unpublished investigations); he attempts, in particular, to complete a system of axioms by adding a separate "axiom of completeness". The above-given analyses should make it evident that, even if the inmost motives that guided him mathematically were inexplicit, they tended essentially in the same direction as those that determined the concept of the definite manifold [definiten Mannigfaltigkeit]. (Husserl 1974, 1969, §31)

Hilbert added the axiom of completeness to the axiomatization of geometry in 1900.[16] In its arithmetical version, the axiom was first stated in *Über den Zahlbegriff* in 1900. This version states that "the numbers form a system of things which is incapable of being extended while continuing to satisfy all the axioms" (Ewald 1996, p. 1094). The axiom posits the categoricity of the system as a maximal system. Whereas Hilbert posited categoricity through maximality, Husserl was motivated by the uniqueness and the related unambiguity of the theory, but arguably also by the "purity" of the domains of categorical theories.

This usage of the term "definiteness" agrees with Husserl's *Prolegomena to the Logical Investigations* (1900) and its definition of a manifold. But around the turn of the century Husserl uses the term "formal bestimmt" for this term and "definit" for what I term "contentual definiteness" to distinguish systematically between the two kinds of definiteness: formal and contentual (Husserl 1975, p. 249, see also 2001d, p. 91).

In *Logical Investigations*, Husserl discussed the idea of logic as it emerges in the practice of mathematics in the nineteenth century. To him the idea of logic comprises three separate tasks: to capture the logical grammar and the corresponding configurations of objects, the theory of validity and the related theories of objects, such as number theory, and finally the theory of theories. The theory of theories is what Husserl thinks that mathematicians as diverse as Riemann, Cantor, Lie, Grassmann, and Hamilton had in mind, even though presumably only implicitly, when they constructed different formal frameworks. Theory of theories is to be a formal theory in which the individual theories and their domains, that is, manifolds, can be examined and related to each other.

Husserl defines a manifold as follows:

> The *objective correlate* of the concept of a possible theory, definite only in respect of form [nur der Form nach bestimmten Theorie], is the concept of a possible *domain of knowledge over which a theory of this form will preside* [durch eine Theorie solcher Form zu beherrschenden Erkenntnisgebietes überhaupt]. Such a domain is, however, known in mathematical circles as a *manifold*. It is accordingly a domain which is uniquely and solely determined by falling under a theory of such a form, whose objects are such as to permit of certain associations which fall under certain basic laws of this or that determinate form (here the only determining feature). The objects remain quite indefinite as regards their matter, to indicate which the mathematician prefers to speak of them as "thought-objects". (Husserl 1975, 2001a, §70, italic in the original)

---

[16] He inserted it into the French translation of *Grundlagen der Geometrie* in 1900, its English translation in 1902 and into the second edition of the work in 1900 (Dreben & Kanamori 1997, p. 84).

This definition is of a *formally* definite manifold as specified in the first line of the quotation: "definite only in respect of form." The formally definite manifold is a unique domain of a theory, its intended model, which is understood as a domain of a categorical theory. As Husserl himself points out, the objects defined by such a theory "remain quite indefinite as regards their matter." Husserl thus sees pure logic as something that encompasses the theory of theories, which in turn is a modern structural enterprise – the Bourbaki group comes immediately to mind. Husserl cited this definition in his *Formal and Transcendental Logic*, suggesting that he still held on to it in the late 1920s. Husserl thus analyzes mathematicians to be naturally *ante rem* structuralists, out to pin down unique structures, such as that of natural numbers (see Shapiro 1997, pp. 84–85, for ante rem structuralism). In a recent work, Tim Button and Sean Walsh (2018) call this kind of view "modelism."[17]

Husserl discussed the notion of "definiteness" in the most detail in the so-called Double Lecture given at two meetings of the Göttingen Mathematical Society in November and December 1901. Husserl starts the lecture with an outline of his general view of mathematics as a structuralist enterprise, a study of manifolds as expressed already in *Prolegomena* (1900). Husserl repeats the view and writes, "the object domain is defined through the axioms in the sense that it is delimited as a certain sphere of objects in general, irrespective of whether real or ideal, for which basic propositions of such and such forms hold true. An object domain thus defined we call a determinate, but formally defined, manifold [bestimmte, aber formal definierte Mannigfaltigkeit]" (Husserl 2001d, p. 91; Husserl 2003, p. 410). Husserl's starting point in the Double Lecture is thus a view of mathematics as a study of manifolds, in particular as a study of *formally definite manifolds*, where formal definiteness refers to, in present terms, domains defined up to isomorphism, that is, domains of categorical theories. (For more detail, see Hartimo 2021a, Chapter 3.)

However, what is notable is that while a kind of structuralism is the starting point for this lecture, Husserl's focus in it is elsewhere, namely, on another, constructive notion of definiteness, that is, contentual definiteness. The motivation for this is in problems that Husserl identifies with the structuralist view: "the difficulties lie precisely in the relationship between formal mathematics

---

[17] Button and Walsh (2018, p. 139) define modelism as "the idea that structure-talk, as used informally by mathematicians, is to be understood in terms of isomorphism, in the model theorist's sense." They distinguish several branches of modelism. Husserl's approach is a species of objects-modelism, according to which 'the natural number structure' really picks out a particular abstract entity, explicated as a particular isomorphism type (2018, p. 144). While model theory did not properly exist during Husserl's time, his view of formally definite manifolds is a structure understood in terms of isomorphism types, similarly to the modelist aspirations in general.

and its employment in substantive mathematics or in the particular domains of knowledge" (Husserl 2001d, p. 92; Husserl 2003, p. 411). Husserl detects the problem to be in the application of these purely formal structures. The application becomes problematic especially if the formal structure includes objects that do not have the corresponding "contentual" counterpart in the particular system (and hence have no real meaning, *Bedeutung*). For example, one would want to operate with negative numerals within the domain of natural numbers, even though they have no reference within the domain. The problem will thus be the usage of what Husserl calls "imaginary" entities, that is, the objects that are added to the domain to facilitate calculations, but which do not have any reference in the original domain. In other words, the problem is that of a conservative extension of a theory, that is, an extension of the original theory, convenient for proving theorems, but which does not prove new theorems about the original theory. Husserl writes,

> An obvious presupposition of the expansion is that the new axiom system be internally consistent. .... But if the new system is a consistent one and includes the old one in itself, then in the entire range of deduction no inconsistency can occur. Thus, a proposition which is somehow derived in such a way that it contains none of the "impossible" forms of operation, cannot possibly include an inconsistency, and thus it is true. (Husserl 2001d, p. 97, 2003, p. 419)

So, Husserl assumes the consistency of the conservative extension of the theory, and hence that the operation with imaginary entities ("imaginary" from the point of view of the original theory) should not produce inconsistencies. But Husserl finds this questionable:

> But how do we know that what is free of contradiction also is true; or as it must be expressed here, how do we know of a proposition that exclusively contains concepts which occur in the narrower domain and are there defined, and which does not conflict with the axioms of the narrower domain, that such a proposition is valid for the narrower domain?" (Husserl 2001d, p. 97, 2003, p. 419)

To overcome this problem, Husserl's aim is then to explain how the corresponding, contentually definite systems can be constructed. If he manages to do this, he writes, the "transition through the imaginary" in the formally definite systems will be possible. The constructibility will show the original domain complete, which then justifies the conservativity of the extension of the domain. It answers Husserl's more philosophical reservations as well: The contentually definite domains are the ones in which the objects are "contentually" determinate, which means, as it turns out, that they have unambiguously determined identities. These are then possible to relate to the objects of intuition, such as numbers thought of as consisting of strings of strokes. Note how Husserl's discussion of conservative extensions anticipates Hilbert's attempts in the 1920s in more than one way: Hilbert not only wanted to base the contentual elementary number theory on a purely intuitive basis of concrete signs, he also sought justification for the theoretical part of mathematics in its conservativity over "real" mathematics, referring to the method of ideal elements:

> In my proof theory, the transfinite axioms and formulae are adjoined to the finite axioms, just as in the theory of complex variables the imaginary elements are adjoined to the real, and just as in geometry the ideal constructions are adjoined to the actual. The motivation and the success of the procedure is the same in my proof theory as it is there: that is, the adjoining of the transfinite axioms results in the simplification and completion of the theory. (Hilbert 1996, p. 1144)

In the Double Lecture, Husserl *constructs* contentually determinate domains with the so-called "existential axioms," with which he establishes the existence of the results of all operations in the system. Note, that the term "axiom" is used in two different senses. The terminology proposed by Solomon Feferman is useful here: Feferman terms the axioms in the old, Aristotelian sense as *foundational* and the Hilbertian axioms with which the formal objects are implicitly defined as *structural* (Feferman 1999). These different senses of the axioms belong to two different styles of doing mathematics around the turn of the century, namely "constructivism" and "postulationism," as they are termed by Ferreirós and Grey (2006, 6–8). Husserl's existential axioms that establish the genuine existence of the objects of the domain are foundational and constructivist. The formal categorical theories are postulational. The axioms in them are structural axioms that implicitly define the formal objects of the domain.

So, with the (foundational) existential axioms Husserl manages to construct an arithmetical or what he also calls "constructive" manifold. These existential axioms are equations that assert an existence of their solution.[18] Husserl claims that these axioms may be univocal or equivocal; that is, they either have one or many solutions. If they are univocal, they have a solution that can be calculated with the rules Husserl gave already in his *Philosophy of Arithmetic* (1891).[19]

---

[18] Here is what Husserl writes about them: "Any axiom system must ... include existence axioms. For example, in the manifold there is to be a combination '+' (which implies that there are to be determinate pairs of elements a b, which are combinable in the form a + b, and 'combinable' means in turn: there is in it at least one new element, which = a + b), and for this combination such and such laws are valid" (Husserl 2001d, p. 98, 2003, p. 420).

[19] Husserl gave step-by-step instructions for addition, multiplication, subtraction, division, and the powers, and so on. After having explained addition, he explained multiplication by means of it, and so forth (Husserl 1970a, pp. 264–283, 2003, pp. 277–296).

In the latter case, "they may be determinately or indeterminately equivocal" (2001d, p. 98, 2003, p. 421). Husserl simply rules out the indeterminately equivocal. The determinate equivocality can be "eliminated by a joint force of the axioms, so that we are enabled univocally to determine new and ever new elements from given elements" (2001d, p. 99, 2003, 421). This is presumably a case where a number is defined by a system of equations, a case likewise discussed already in *Philosophy of Arithmetic* (1970a, pp. 281–282, 2003, pp. 297–298).

Husserl thus uses his view of calculation defined in *Philosophy of Arithmetic* already in 1891. According to him, calculation is "any rule-governed mode of derivation for signs from signs within any algorithmic sign-system according to the 'laws' – or better – conventions – for combination, separation, and transformation peculiar to that system" (1970a, p. 258, 2003, p. 273). Likewise, Husserl held that the general postulate of arithmetic is the following:

> the symbolic formations that are different from the systematic numbers [i.e., numerals given with the decimal system, considered as numbers] must, wherever they turn up, be reduced to the systematic numbers equivalent to them, as their normative forms. Accordingly there arises, as the *first basic task of Arithmetic, to separate all conceivable symbolic modes of formation of numbers into their distinct types, and to discover for each type the methods that are reliable and as simple as possible for carrying out that reduction.* (Husserl 1970a, p. 262, 2003, p. 277, italic in the original)

So, Husserl is in principle discussing what he calls formations of different types: 18 + 49 is a formation of a sum, 7 * 36 is a formation of a multiplication (his examples, cf. 1970a, p. 261, 2003, p. 276). The first step is to identify the type in question (whether a sum, multiplication, and so forth). Then one needs to perform the calculations according to the given rules. This enables calculating different "formations" so that ultimately univocal results, located in the number sequence, are obtained. Husserl is thus describing a system that is decidable as a terminating term-rewriting structure: all terms are reducible to natural numbers. And, these manifolds are clearly intuitable because all the steps are intuitable: "We clarify the concept $(5^3)^4$ by having recourse to the definitory presentation: number which arises when one forms the product $(5^3) \times (5^3) \times (5^3) \times (5^3)$. If we wish to clarify this latter concept, we must go back to the sense of (5^3), i.e. to the formation 5×5×5. Going back further, we should have to clarify 5 through the definitory chain 5=4 +1, 4=3+1, 3=2+1, 2=1+1" as Husserl puts it in the Sixth Logical Investigation (1984, p. 601, 2001b, pp. 229–230). This gives an answer to why Husserl thinks these numbers actually exist, for he thinks this makes numbers fully intuitive: after a finite number of steps, the series ends up in an immediate intuition.

Thus, to put it briefly, in Husserl's view around the turn of the century, there is postulational mathematics where the manifolds may be, or ideally are, formally definite. These formally definite manifolds are domains of categorical theories, and formally definite theories are categorical theories. For the sake of application and to show that they actually exist, they should be "filled in," that is, made determinate with the previously described "contentual" and decidable concrete construction. Husserl does this by means of equational systems that, if definite, can be reduced in stepwise computations to natural numbers or even further to sums of 1 that are immediately intuited. Today it is known that such contentually definite manifolds are computationally complete thanks to their decidable re-writing structure. Thus, they manage to justify the condition needed to establish conservativity of the extension of the manifold and hence they justify the usage of the imaginaries (cf. Okada 2013, Hartimo & Okada 2018, Hartimo 2021a, Chapter 3). Moreover, they also show how to relate arithmetic to intuition, and hence it could be taken as "true" and not merely non-contradictory.

What I want to emphasize here is that Husserl's *Besinnung* of the mathematicians in the nineteenth century includes both the postulational and constructive styles of doing mathematics. These are characterized by different goals: one is categoricity; the other is to be determinate in terms of content. Husserl analyses the latter as being constructively built from below up and as mechanically reducible to natural numbers.

2.1.1 Foundational Debates after 1902 and Husserl's Reaction

In Husserl's texts after the Double Lecture one can detect further analysis of these two mathematical attitudes guided by different ideals, namely, categoricity and constructivism and decidability. These two attitudes can also be detected in the foundational debates after Russell discovered the paradox in Frege's concept-script. While Zermelo axiomatized set theory and proposed the axiom of separation in place of Cantor's naïve comprehension axiom, Poincaré demanded predicative foundations. Brouwer then sharpened his views regarding the constructive method required in mathematics and suggested that the classical principles of logic are unreliable.[20] The year 1908 was particularly interesting from this point of view: Brouwer published "The Untrustworthiness of Logical Principles," in which he discussed a constructive

---

[20] To be sure, a similar debate took place already in the nineteenth century between Dedekind and Kronecker. However, at that point Husserl, a student of Weierstrass and Kronecker, had not yet developed the view he held from the turn of the century onward. At the end of the nineteenth century, he adopted the structuralist view of modern mathematics (without referring to Dedekind) and complemented it with his earlier somewhat constructivist views. This development is related to his turn toward anti-psychologism and the demand for "theoretical" foundations for normative logic.

approach and equated the law of the excluded middle with the question of whether there may be unsolvable mathematical problems. During the same year, in his axiomatization of set theory, Zermelo postulated the axiom of separation: "Whenever the propositional function $\mathfrak{E}$ (x) is definite for all elements of a set M, M possesses a subset $M_{\mathfrak{E}}$ containing as elements precisely those elements x of M for which $\mathfrak{E}$ (x) is true" (1908, p. 202). In contrast to Cantor's naïve comprehension, the axiom of separation takes care of the Zermelo-Russell paradoxes by separating sets from already defined sets so that there can be no universal sets.

Husserl was involved in the debate about the paradoxes as well. He exchanged letters with Frege on the topic in 1906 and 1907. In his notes on various paradoxes, dated mainly to 1912, he held that the paradoxes resulted from the usage of terms whose meanings have shifted and hence are not clear and distinct. Given the shortage of materials about the matter, we can only speculate what Husserl could have meant by this: Did he think that the definitions should be predicative, or did he perhaps just mean that one should abandon naïve comprehension? In these lectures Husserl also wonders whether the concept of set is essentially dependent on the notion of definite manifold, which is equally ambiguous (Ierna & Lohmar 2016, Rosado Haddock 2006). In any case, I contend that such problems led him to focus on judgments and an attempt at generalizing the arithmetical attitude of the Double Lecture with a judgment-theoretical account that he developed on the basis of his discussions of grammar in *The Logical Investigations*.

Hence, in *Ideas I*, published in 1913, Husserl offers a detailed account of discernment of essences in judgments: in §1, he explains how to each science there corresponds a region of objects as its domain. These objects have an essence, which is discerned in judgments. The objects are thus subjects of possible, true predications. In §5, Husserl introduces "'axioms,' immediately evident judgments to which, indeed, all other judgments lead back in a mediated justification" (Husserl 1976a, 2014, §5). These immediately evident judgments are axioms in a foundational sense, like the existential axioms discussed earlier in connection with Husserl's Double Lecture. All other judgments are built upon them, and I read the "leading back" as mechanical reducibility to the evident foundational judgments. Husserl's aim is to give a schema "*in terms of which it is possible necessarily to determine individuals under 'synthetic principles a priori' according to concepts and laws, or to ground all empirical sciences necessarily on regional ontologies pertaining to them and not merely on the pure logic common to all sciences*" (Husserl 1976a, 2014, §17, italic in the original). The theory built up by the (foundational) axioms is thus *a synthetic a priori theory* as opposed to the pure logic (understood in Husserl's sense, encompassing postulational formal mathematics, which uses axioms structurally), common to all sciences. In terms of the previous section, Husserl's schema is supposed to be contentually definite, that is, provide full determination of the individuals of the domain by constructing them. The difference to the previous attempt is that now he does it in a linguistic context of theory of judgments. Note that this does not mean giving up on the idea of pure logic common to all sciences. Thus, he maintains the postulational, pure approach as well.

2.1.2 Lectures on Logic and General Theory of Science

Between 1910 and 1918 Husserl lectured four times on logic and general theory of science in Göttingen and Freiburg. The last version of the lecture course, given in 1917–18 in Freiburg, is published as volume 30 of the Husserliana series (Husserl 1996) and translated by Claire Hill as Collected Works, volume XV (Husserl 2019).[21] The lecture notes are divided into three sections, where the first is titled "Fundamental considerations for the demarcation and characterization of formal logic," the second, "The systematic theory of forms of meanings and of judgment," and the third "The general idea of the theory of science."

The third and last section of Husserl's 1918 lecture course is particularly pertinent for the present purpose. It contains the general idea (goal) of the theory of science, "the governing idea for the entire content of my lectures" (1996, 2019, §54). Here Husserl discusses formally definite manifolds, that is, "disciplines of exactly the same form" (1996, 2019, §54), that is, discipline-forms – in the present-day vocabulary the categorical theories or isomorphism types.[22] Husserl exemplifies the idea by discussing Euclidean geometry, eventually perfected by Hilbert (1996, 2019, §55). Husserl contrasts this with what he thinks is the most obvious procedure, that is, the one that begins with a few pure concepts "straight line," "angle," "plane," and so on, in order to establish directly intuitable axioms [apriorische und unmittelbar einsichtige Axiome] (thus foundational axioms). "Then, one draws in, for instance, new concepts and new directly evident concept-propositions and advances again on to new, no longer obvious, ones by drawing inferences out of those already established"

---

[21] The course was first held in Göttingen in winter semester 1910/11 entitled *Logik als Theorie der Erkenntnis*, then during the winter semesters 1912/13 and 1914/15 under the title *Logik und Einleitung in die Wissenschaftslehre*, and finally in Freiburg in 1917/18 under the present title, that is, *Logik und Allgemeine Wissenschaftstheorie* (Hill 2019, p. xxiii)

[22] Button and Walsh (2018, p. 38) explicate structures by isomorphism types, that is, classes of isomorphic models.

(1996, 2019, §55). This latter procedure seems to exemplify Husserl's bottom-up view of the constructive judgment theory.

The formal definiteness still looms in the background. Husserl explains the nature of the discipline-systems in detail in §56, and explains, for example, their usefulness in that by dealing with one discipline-form, one can obtain results that hold in all domains of the same form. He then poses again the problem about using the imaginary. In addition to what he explained in the Double Lecture he now has added the requirement of the grammatical meaningfulness of the language of the theory. He also points out that "not every formally thrown together system of axiom-forms allows one to define a discipline-form that is complete in this respect" (1996, 2019, §56). In other words, he explicitly admits that not all theories are categorical.

In §57 Husserl explains that the problem of freely operating

> leads to systematically broadening the definite discipline-forms and to pursuing [*nachzugehen*] all possibilities of the construction of definite discipline-forms. Correlatively corresponding to each such discipline-form there is an object-domain conceived in indeterminate universality that is fully indeterminate in terms of content and only receives more precise determination through those combinations [*Verknüpfungen*] of categorial concepts that are present in the axiom-forms. (translation modified Husserl 1996, 2019, §57)

The discipline-forms relate to objects conceived in indeterminate universality, the structuralist objects as they are. Formulated in more contemporary terminology, they are objects defined solely by the place they have in the structure. Husserl writes: "After formalization, the words 'point,' 'straight line,' 'angle,' 'intersect,' and so forth are completely empty signs that only have the purely formal meaning that the axiom-form prescribes for them" and then he continues to point out that "the definition of a manifold as Euclidean does not state anything about existence any more than the definition of a golden mountain does about [a] mountain made of gold" (1996, 2019, §57). He nevertheless goes on to ascribe some *being* to the Euclidean manifold, namely mere formal being [*sein*] of analytic concord. Such discipline-forms or axiom-forms defining the manifold can then be varied in different directions, such as in terms of dimensions or curvature. "And all these infinite manifolds are characterized by common properties, for example, by the fact that in them every configuration can 'shift' within the manifold without 'straining' and 'distortion,' where 'shifting' ('straining,' 'distortion') is obviously a purely formal concept, a formal generalization of what we know in space as movement" (1996, 2019, §57). In a glance, with it, we "survey infinities of possible discipline-forms, or infinities of manifolds defined by axiom systems and explore the laws governing in the relationships and variations of manifolds ... a supreme consummation of analytics" (1996, 2019, §57). Husserl points out that this is not a matter of a mere game, but "of a sphere of insights worthy of the highest theoretical interest" (1996, 2019, §57).

But this is not the entire *mathesis universalis*. After having explained the usefulness and interest of the formal axiomatic, that is, postulational, attitude Husserl then moves on to discuss the need for the actual, or more concrete formal domains, what he called "synthetic a priori schemata" in *Ideas I*. (I assume that in the indented quotation earlier, the last sentence refers to the way more concreteness to the discipline-form is given by means of the combination of concepts within the theory of judgments.) He first complains that mathematicians disregard the difference between the arithmetic of cardinal numbers, the arithmetic of ordinal numbers, and the different kinds of arithmetic of large numbers. The complaint may seem unfair, but Husserl's point is to draw attention to the *contentual* differences between these different systems disregarded in structuralist mathematics. He holds that mathematicians "overlook a step in reasoning, namely, just that of the application, of subsumption" (1996, 2019, §59). An ideal *mathesis universalis* includes all the "direct law-truths," hence the direct (foundational) axioms of cardinal numbers or ordinal numbers, and so forth, in which the axioms are laid down step by step. To avoid vicious circles, the actual theories should be constructed systematically, so that they start with completely direct axioms. After this, "[e]ach step of indirect thinking that it takes must be directly perspicuous. It is only valid if its law is valid" (1996, 2019, §59).

The ideal *mathesis universalis*, according to Husserl thus includes the foundational axioms and the domain that is built up from below. In particular, the full *mathesis universalis* includes the deductive proofs of the theorems. Indeed, earlier in the lecture course Husserl discussed the concept of proof. He explained that a proof consists of inferences that are direct and perpicacious [unmittelbar einsichtig].[23] (§49) He thought, for example, that "the whole proof – as many partial inferences as it contains, with the judgments constructing it – is obviously a judgment-unit. It can be looked upon as a judgment" (2019, §49). He also points out that "a deductive theory is no more than a web of proofs by means of which an essentially related group of truths leads back to one

---

[23] Husserl writes, in 1918, that "Superfluous premises will not be tolerated in a proof. What is not necessary for the argumentation is a hindrance and must remain struck out. So, one will not, so to speak, go round in circles and want to advance from equivalent to equivalent, introducing new terms and then eliminating them again, without anything essentially new resulting. In this way, whole portions of the proof can be superfluous, which would be a flaw in the proof" (2019, pp. 258–259). Husserl then formalizes, in Schröder's notation, a proof in which he uses the cut rule twice. He formulates the cut rule thus much earlier than for example Paul Hertz who used it in 1922 (von Plato 2017, 266).

and the same store of basic truths as the consistently perfect irreducible basis out of which they are all provable and by this means are (as people also say) explained" (2019, §50). In other words, the full *mathesis* includes the theory of judgments, which in turn includes the perspicious proofs of the theorems. Husserl concludes his discussion of proofs by pointing out that he is not going to engage in a detailed construction of this theory because

> the construction of these theories and theoretical disciplines is in my opinion not a matter for philosophers, but a matter for mathematicians. Just as from time immemorial, arithmetic, and since the Renaissance, algebra and analysis, as against philosophy, have developed as independent sciences, so they must also remain independent. . . . In my opinion, all polemicizing against mathematizing logic testifies to a lack of understanding. Constructing deductive theories is definitely the business of mathematicians. (2019, p. 262)

In other words, Husserl does not claim to be a proof theorist himself; his discussion of the concept of proof appears to be based on the findings in the algebra of logic tradition, and presumably Schröder in particular. I take this to be an indication of Husserl's *Besinnung* of the mathematicians in Göttingen, such as Bernays (who was in Göttingen in 1912 and then 1917–33) and Skolem (who was in Göttingen in 1915–16).[24] The notion of contentual definiteness is eventually captured by Oskar Becker in his Habilitationsschrift, *Beiträge zur phänomenologschen Begründung der Geometrie und ihrer physicaliscen Anwendungen* supervised by Husserl and published in Husserl's Jahrbuch in 1923 as follows: "Definiteness, . . ., means that *all* possible formations of the subject area in question can be reached by an algorithm consisting of a finite number of basic elements, and further that the [con]structive complication of the algorithm does not become infinite" (Becker 1923, p. 402, italic in the original. My attention to this passage is due Wachtel 2024, p. 191). In his attempts of formulating contentual definiteness Husserl seems to have had in mind the concept of effective method that was made precise by Turing and Church in 1936, but what was "in the air" in various ways, implicitly guiding one strand in the development of mathematics in Göttingen already in the early decades of the twentieth century.

Both, the bottom-up judgment theory and the top-down axiomatics continue to characterize Husserl's writings throughout the 1920s. For example, in a lecture course from 1926, Husserl writes: "The world can be regarded in two ways: as the world of exact realities and exact wholes, and as the world of

---

[24] (von Plato 2017, pp. 86–93). Jan von Plato summarizes Skolem's approach in 1919 as follows: "*Decidability is the only criterion of existence. All decision procedures have to terminate in a bounded number of steps*" (2017, p. 143, italic in the original). This resonates perfectly with Husserl's view of contentual definiteness.

morphological realities and morphological wholes" (Husserl 2012, pp. 262–263). He then explains that the morphological (descriptive) attitude starts by looking at objects from a specific point of view and classifying them under types of different levels. In his view, the world is given in a morphological structure that is finitely verifiable and bound to a historical situation (Husserl 2012, pp. 273, 285–290). Yet, Husserl holds that "behind" the intuited reality, there is the exact world that has an infinite, mathematical, Euclidean structure (Husserl 2012, p. 290). Similarly in 1927:

> Every possible world therefore has a double a priori. A formal-mathematical one, insofar as the world with its infinities is conceived in empty formal generality (in our sense analytically) as a mathematical manifold under abstraction from all that is factually determining. But it also has its universal and concrete factual a priori, which, in unity [in eins] with the analytical one, can precede [vorangehen kann] every research into experience and, if it is scientifically construed [gefasst], can serve it as an instrument of method. In this sense, all natural science is based on formal and material mathematics . . . (Husserl 2001c, p. 44; translation by author)

In this quotation, Husserl uses the term "material" where I think the more correct term would be "contentual" in order to save "material" for domain specific use that is informed by experience, where domains are not mathematically defined (as in Schröder), but empirical, such as human, organic and inorganic beings (I will elaborate on this in the next section). All this shows how Husserl engages in *Besinnung* of the mathematicians of his time. He does not postulate what mathematics should be like but detects the two styles of doing mathematics: the constructive and the postulational. He presumably would conclude, in agreement with Bernays who wrote about a decade later, that "the two tendencies, intuitionist and platonist, are both necessary; they complement each other, and it would be doing oneself violence to renounce one or the other" (1935, p. 269). And, like Bernays (1935, p. 267), Husserl thinks that the chosen method depends on the character of the object investigated as explained in Section 2.2.1.

2.1.3 Formal and Transcendental Logic

Formal and Transcendental Logic (1929) wraps things up, and as a published book, should be regarded as Husserl's last and best-thought-out analysis of the formal sciences. The book explicitly uses the method of radical *Besinnung* to carry out a historical sense-investigation of the exact sciences. Husserl's treatment thus repeats the bifurcated nature of the constructive judgment theory and structuralist "postulational" mathematics present from his Double Lecture onward. Husserl's main concern now is to see how the two trends are related and how they require what he calls "transcendental logic."

Husserl first traces the development of logic from Aristotle, through the emergence of algebra, to his own concept of the formal theory of judgments. The primitive form of the theory of judgment is the traditional one: "S is p," where S refers to a substrate and p to a determination. From this primitive form of judgment further derived forms can be constructed. Husserl's examples are "Sp is q," "(Sp)q is r," and so forth, or modifications like "if S is p" or "then S is q" that can be combined into judgment-forms. He refers to these acts as *construction* [*Konstruktion*], with which one can derive particularizations and modifications from the primitive forms, such as "S is p" (§13b). It should be noted that despite using the traditional form of judgment, the judgment theory not only includes traditional syllogistics but, importantly, it also covers all acts made in modern mathematics (see Klev 2017, for a detailed account of Husserl's grammar). Hence, for example, it includes relations, which "traditional logic is unwilling to admit" as Russell puts it (Russell 1903, §208).

Given his awareness of the development of logic, Husserl's decision to rely on the traditional form of judgment may appear puzzling. The earlier discussion hopefully at least partly explains Husserl's obliviousness to the modern form of judgment in his genesis of logic. There are many other reasons for it, too: Originally Husserl wanted to avoid set theoretical paradoxes with his careful analysis of a judgment. The traditional form of judgment captures the intentional directedness to the objects in the judgments. It reflects the way we are ordinarily occupied by objects and their determinations (cf. Cobb-Stevens 1990, p. 145). Thus, it enables capturing the epistemological, "seeing-as" aspect, that is, how the objects are determined in certain ways. It also facilitates the bottom-up idea in constructing theories on the basis of the evidence of the objects that are judged about. And finally, the form of judgment will also be formally useful as we will soon see (it enables decidability of the judgment theory), although this idea was developed only later and was unavailable to Husserl. The development of theory of judgments is guided by three different goals: grammaticality, non-contradiction, and truth. These goals are associated with three different kinds of evidence: evidence of grammaticality, distinctness, and clarity that serve as norms for scientific discourse.

Husserl's historical sense-investigation of mathematics, in turn, starts with Euclid and culminates in Riemann and Hilbert. The concept of definite manifolds is the clarification of this development. Husserl's structuralism is unchanged in *Formal and Transcendental Logic*; in other words, categoricity is still the ideal goal of mathematics. Mathematicians, in Husserl's view, are still (in 1929) "modelists" about the theory of arithmetic to use Button and Walsh's terminology. They think that the theory of arithmetic picks out, or at least should pick out, a particular equivalence class of isomorphic models. To be sure, this does not rule them out to be algebraists about other theories (cf. Button and Walsh 2018, p. 38).

In *Formal and Transcendental Logic*, Husserl argues that on the analytic level, that is, when looking at these disciplines formally, in detachment from how they can be applied to the world, formal judgment theory and formal mathematics ultimately refer to one discipline. Both can be developed analytically, that is, non-contradictorily, within the evidence of distinctness. However, the two disciplines have different purposes, which creates tension between them: Whereas categoricity is the guiding idea of modern structural mathematics, the theory of judgment is in addition governed by the norm of truth: it should reveal the laws of truth, it should be about the world. The theory of judgments should be applicable to the world, which is not a concern in pure mathematics. Because of its ultimate directedness to be about experienced objects and their determinations, the theory of judgments is also more explicit about contentual differences among theories. The guiding goal of the judgment theory is, arguably, to be contentually definite, which requires it to be constructive and decidable. The subsequent transcendental analyses make this even clearer.

2.1.4 The "Transitional Link" and Relatedness of Logic to Objects of Experiences

In his transcendental analysis of the conditions of possibility of these formal theories, Husserl clarifies the nature of judgment-theory in a way that shows its goal to offer computable determination and definiteness in terms of *decidability* (i.e., there is a procedure by which the complex expression can be reduced in a series of computable steps to an elementary one). The judgment-theory is a decidable fragment of the more encompassing theory of judgments that encompasses all of mathematics. The context for the discussion about judgment-theory is Husserl's attempt to explicate the network of different kinds of evidence and their hierarchy, that is, how one kind of evidence is more primary than another. Husserl offers a decidable judgment-theory as a heuristic device for this work. He discusses it as a "transitional link" between the pure logic of non-contradiction and truth-logic. Since Husserl refuses to count it as either – either as logic of non-contradiction or as truth-logic, he seems to think of it as some kind of auxiliary help, a technique, with which to draw contours of evidence.

In what follows, I try to form an understanding of how the "transitional link" could be considered to be located between the logic of non-contradiction and the logic of truth. I will start with a consideration of the formality of formal mathematics. Ideally, in formal mathematics, objects are characterized structuralistically as discussed earlier. The formal objects are determined formally by the relations they have to each other or to the theory. In terms of matter, they are entirely indeterminate. Husserl calls them "empty anything-whatevers" (1974, 1969, §29). "Formality" in this context means indeterminacy, but not lacking in stuff. Thus, formal mathematics has content, stuff, but this content is entirely indeterminate.

The theory of judgments is about formal objects, which are likewise "anything whatevers" but instead of being completely indeterminate they assume grammatical types. They are determined with grammatical forms, that is, they are substantives, adjectives, or relatives, and so forth. These forms may be complex, that is, they may be composed of other forms. Ultimately, however, the complex forms are reducible to the ultimate subjects, predicates, universalities, and relations. This reduction is mechanical, Husserl writes, that it takes place "purely by following up the meanings." In other words, the complex judgments are mechanically reducible to elementary judgments (1974, 1969, §82).

With the hindsight of later developments in formal logic, it can be remarked that this kind of reducibility would be possible also on the level of non-contradiction if the "empty" somethings had, not only grammatical determination, but also some further contentual determination so as to have enough "computable" content to enable the mechanical reduction to the primitive forms. This means that the judgment-theory should also explicate the types of the (otherwise) empty somethings to acquire fuller contentual determinateness. This is the case in the intuitionistic type theory (developed by Per Martin-Löf since the 1970s), which is in this sense decidable and which also uses the traditional form of judgment. In it the computable content is due to so-called Curry-Howard isomorphism, according to which propositions are viewed as types (for more detail about it, see Crosilla 2022, Dybjer and Palmgren 2020). It thus serves as a paradigm for how the judgment theory could be developed in practice. The types in intuitionistic type theory are formal in the sense that they do not refer to empirical subject matter. For this reason, I have chosen to call the determinateness in this case "contentual" instead of material (as I did before). For the same reason, I believe, Husserl calls the judgment theory a "transitional link," for it is not entirely formal, its contents are not completely indeterminate, but it is not about empirical matters and hence of truth, because it is still entirely a priori, even if "synthetic a priori" as Husserl called it in *Ideas I*. But, Husserl writes, formal logic "is intended to serve the ends of sciences that have material content. Thus, the ultimate applicability of formal analytics to individuals is, at the same time, a teleological relatedness to all possible spheres of individuals"

(1974, 1969, §83). Formal logic has the contentual structure that anticipates how it could become a logic of truth, which would then be about the world.

The truth-logic is ultimately about the objects of perception or memory which fall into material types. In other words, the empirical categories, such as biological categories, like different species, would add to the truth-logic material determinateness, which would be specific to different regions. In a sense, contentual definiteness seeks to spell out the decidable contentual scaffolding of any domain (a kind of formal ontology). On the top of it, the material definiteness seeks to give the domain specific material determination so that these specific material determinations lead to material ontologies. This I think explains why the judgment-theory is "transitional" between pure theories of mathematics and the logic of truth.[25]

2.1.5 Conclusion: Structuralist Form and Constructivist Formal Content

To conclude this section, let us summarize the argument made so far: Husserl's investigation of mathematical practice of his time identifies in it two goals: the domains should be characterized with formal definiteness – with categorical theories – and also with contentual definiteness, which demands decidable contentual construction. Husserl examines the genesis of these two aspects as a mathematical and a judgment-theoretical development, respectively. The difference between the two is in the kinds of evidence they aim at. The mathematical attitude is in Husserl's sense analytic; that is, it is formal, with non-contradiction as its necessary condition, and distinctness as the intended kind of evidence. The judgment-theoretical attitude can be viewed analytically as well, but its ultimate sense is to be applicable to the world so that it provides the "synthetic principles a priori" for the purposes of empirical sciences.

Already on the analytic level, guided by the evidence of distinctness, the apophantic, judgment-theoretical attitude adds contentual determination to the otherwise formal attitude of structural mathematics. Husserl thinks that mathematicians in their "modelist" aspiration to pin down unique structures overlook the contentual differences between various attitudes. In *Formal and Transcendental Logic*, he claims that the judgment-theory uncovers "hidden intentional implications" in the judgments made in mathematics (§§85–87). Husserl analyzes the contentual determination mainly as grammatical determination (substantives, adjectives, relations, etc.). However, for a system to be mechanically reducible to the elementary judgments in the way Husserl wanted it to be, this contentual determination has to include more "computable" content than what Husserl

---

[25] Additional support for this interpretation can be found in Husserl's views about formal ontology (such as 1974, 1969, §54; see also Hartimo 2020b).

identifies. This is the case with intuitionistic type theory that – I suggest – serves as a paradigm for the desired kind of judgment-theory. Using the traditional form of judgment, it explains what is meant by construction and what a constructive mathematical object is, thus clarifying Husserl's somewhat vague intuitions about contentual definiteness.

When judgments additionally have material content and are about the world, the guiding evidence is that of clarity, obtained from encountering matters themselves. The judgment-theory shows the genesis of the complex judgments from the primitive ones. Hence it is needed for understanding how the exact sciences point back to judgments about individuals in experiential judgments, that is, judgments about possible perception and memory. The judgment-theory is thus meant to show how formal theories are ultimately founded (grounded?) on judgments of perception. Going the other way around, from the perceptual judgments up to formal theories, shows the various ways of abstraction needed to reach the purely formal theories.

2.2 Transcendental Investigation of the Goals of Mathematical Practices

Having described the practice of mathematics in terms of its goals, Husserl turns his attention to examining the transcendental conditions of this practice as indicated in Section 1.3. And as already noted, he describes this proceeding as follows:

> Turning reflectively from the only themes given straight-forwardly (which may become importantly shifted) to the activity constituting them with its aiming and fulfilment – the activity that is hidden (or, as we may also say, "anonymous") throughout the naïve doing and only now becomes a theme in its own right – we examine that activity after the fact. That is to say, we *examine the evidence* awakened by our reflection, *we ask it what it was aiming at and what it acquired*; and, in the evidence belonging to a higher level, we identify and fix, or we trace, the possible variations owing to vacillations of theme that had previously gone unnoticed, and distinguish the corresponding aimings and actualizations, – in other words, the shifting processes of forming concepts that pertain to logic. (Husserl 1974, 1969, §69, italic in the original)

The purpose of the transcendental examination is to make the "hidden" subject-ive "structuring," or transcendental conditions of possibility explicit so that possible conceptual confusions could be corrected. This means turning to the constitution of mathematics and logic (theory of judgments) and the three different kinds of evidence aimed at in them, that is, grammaticality, distinct-ness, and clarity (Husserl 1974, 1969, §70a). The decidable judgment-theory has a role here: it explicates the structures that are left entirely indeterminate in the purely formal attitude. It also explains how, on the level of distinctness as well as of clarity, the more complex judgments are reducible to the elementary judgments. In doing that, it shows how, in return, evidence can be mediated and thus passed on to the more abstract parts of mathematics.

The transcendental examination brings to light a number of idealizing presuppositions of logic. As already mentioned in passing, we are, for example, able to make the same judgment repeatedly, which presupposes an ideal identity of judgments. Mathematics presupposes that different people at different times can make the same judgment and use the same concepts. The made judgments are further thought to exist at all times, and available to us at all times "as convictions lasting for us from the time of their first constitution" (1974, 1969, §73). Mathematics also presupposes infinite reiterability or that "one can always again" with which one can always form "another set, which is excluded from a given set, and join it to the latter by addition" or one can form the infinite series of cardinal numbers (1974, 1969, §74). Husserl points out that "[t]his is plainly an idealization, since de facto no one can always again" (§74). Husserl also mentions as presuppositions the logical principles such as the law of contradiction and the law of the excluded middle (§§75–77, I will discuss them in more detail shortly); *modus ponens* (§78), and the fundamental presupposition that every judgment can be decided. Husserl holds that every scientist is guided by a fundamental conviction that there is truth in itself and falsity in itself, and this is a condition of possibility of scientific enterprises. Husserl thus seems to hold that truth-value realism is a transcendental condition of scientific practice. This does not mean that the judgments are decided in practice: "For *us*, the legitimacy of many judgments remains undecided. And for us, most of the judgments that are somehow possible can never be evidently decided *in fact*; but in themselves, they can be. *In itself every judgment is decided*" (§79, italic in the original). Husserl further specifies that this means decided by a method, "by a course of cognitive thinking, a course existing in itself and intrinsically pursuable, which leads immediately or mediately to an adequation, a making evident of either the truth or the falsity of any judgment" (§79). A charitable way of looking at these claims is that Husserl is not talking about the decidable judgment-theory but the more encompassing theory of judgments which covers all acts in mathematics. Thus his view here is like Gödel's: "it turns out that in the systematic establishment of the axioms of mathematics, new axioms, which do not follow by formal logic from those previously established, again and again become evident. It is not at all excluded by the negative results mentioned earlier that nevertheless every clearly posed mathematical yes-or-no question is solvable in this way. For it is just this becoming evident of more and more new axioms on the basis of the meaning of the primitive notions that a machine cannot imitate" (1961, 385).

As we saw, the judgment-theory takes us ultimately to judgments about individuals in experiential judgments which are judgments about data of possible perception and memory. Thus, the judgment theory takes us to general phenomenology of intersubjective consciousness and the pre-predicative experiences examined in *Experience and Judgment*. This is a study of the irreducibly first-personal passive undergirding of all our experiences and the transcendental condition of the possibility of making judgments in general and hence of logic and mathematics in particular. For this reason, Husserl eventually claims "that nothing exists for me otherwise than by virtue of the *actual and potential performance of my own consciousness*" (§94, italic in the original). This is not a statement of naïve idealism, but a claim about the necessary condition for having experiences: in order to have experiences we have to be alive and conscious.

2.2.1 Logical Principles

In both *Prolegomena to the Logical Investigations* and *Formal and Transcendental Logic*, Husserl discusses normative logical principles, which determine what is allowed or what is not allowed to be inferred in different theories. These are principles such as the law of the excluded middle, which is particularly interesting because its acceptance distinguishes classical logic from intuitionistic logic.

In *Formal and Transcendental Logic* these principles are revealed by transcendental investigation. In other words, Husserl assumes that the "formal" theories, as discussed up to now, are informal in the sense that the deductions from the axioms of the theories to the theorems are not formalized. Consequently, one needs to examine these theories transcendentally to detect what kinds of logical principles hold in them. One may also wonder if the judgment theory should be consulted here or not. Husserl does not, at least not explicitly, do so.

In *Formal and Transcendental Logic*, Husserl discusses the presupposed logical principles separately for the formal theories governed by distinctness (logic of non-contradiction), and for the formal theories that also aim at clarity, that is (empirical or non-empirical) adequacy (i.e., logic of truth). He seems to think that the same principles are valid in both realms, that of distinctness and of truth. However, Husserl examines these separately. And he holds that without such examination the logical principles may be applied mistakenly: "Because of the formal abstractness and naïveté of the logician's thinking, such never-formulated presuppositions can easily be overlooked;

and consequently a false range can be attributed even to the fundamental concepts and principles of logic" (§80). Accordingly, in a manuscript from 1926 Husserl held that it is a transcendental problem whether the law of the excluded middle holds with regard to the *organic* world (Husserl 2012, p. 301).

All this suggests that Husserl does not think like Frege that there is one true logic that governs absolutely everything. For Frege the laws of logic are "the most general laws, which prescribe universally the way in which one ought to think if one is to think at all" (1893, p. xv, translation from Beaney 1997, p. 202). Husserl thinks that this kind of generality cannot be taken for granted and his view is more in line with Bernays (1935, see the end of Section 2.1.2). Accordingly, Husserl also criticizes Kant for not having raised transcendental questions about logic (1969, §100). For him, logic is not in this sense special among the sciences even though it is a priori (and hence not continuous with science). It should not be dogmatically assumed but it too requires transcendental reflection. For him, it seems, the correctness of the logical principles depends on the enterprise in question (aiming at truth or mere non-contradiction) and on the nature of the subject matter.

This approach seems to lead the Husserlian of the twenty-first century to hold that the choice of logic depends on transcendental reflection about which principles are found to be valid for a given enterprise in a given domain. Transcendental reflection should be able to accommodate either intuitionistic or classical principles, or any logic for that matter, depending on the sphere of application, such as the size of the domain, and our goals and epistemic values that determine what kinds of proofs or definitions we are after. Indeed, I believe the Husserlian view of logic in the twenty-first century is pluralist, and one which obtains its normative status from underlying practices (cf., Kouri-Kissel & Shapiro 2020). All this however requires a prior discussion of what exactly "phenomenological philosophy" or the "Husserlian view" is if it is not something directly drawn from Husserl's texts. This problem will be addressed in the last section of this Element, and a more detailed discussion of the phenomenological view of logic is then deferred to another occasion.

2.2.2 What Is the Mathematical Reality Like for the Mathematicians?

In everyday life as well as in science, "experience is the consciousness of being with the matters themselves, of seizing upon and having them quite directly," Husserl writes (§94). We are in the world, which we do not experience as being behind a veil of appearances. The aim of transcendental phenomenology is to explicate the passive and active constitution that makes such direct experience of the matters themselves possible. Thanks to its metaphysical neutrality, the phenomenological method aims to characterize exhaustively, but without adding anything extra to it, the way the world is constituted in the examined kind of experience. This includes a description of whether the given object is experienced as imagined, as existing, as remembered, etc. As argued in the first section, the metaphysical neutrality of the method has metaphysical implications in that it explicates what kind of metaphysical view is implicit in the practice in question and how it is constituted. As Husserl puts it in *Formal and Transcendental Logic*,

> [e]xperience is the performance in which for me, the experiencer, experienced being "is there," and is there *as what* it is, with the whole content and the mode of being that experience itself, by the performance going on in its intentionality, attributes it. If what is experienced has the sense of *"transcendent" being*, then it is the experiencing that constitutes this sense, and does so either by itself or in the whole motivational nexus pertaining to it and helping to make up its intentionality. (Husserl 1974, 1969, §94, italic in the original)[26]

Describing the givenness of the objects is tantamount to describing the constitution of the object. The constitution is the performance in which the object is (passively or actively) synthesized to what is given in experience.[27] And as we know (from our experience), our experiences are informed by our background knowledge, the results of empirical probing (such as trying to find out by hand whether the stick half in water is bent or not), and empirical investigations, which all belong to the motivational nexus mentioned in the earlier quotation. We naturally view the world rather holistically: we derive, from various kinds of sensory input, data with which we seek to form a harmonious view of the world; we do this on various levels of intersubjectivity, and ultimately even construct scientific methods to investigate the world in specific ways in more detail. The transcendental attitude describes thus the constitution of this direct realism (hence Richard Tieszen (2011) called it constituted platonism). Our world also includes abstract objects, so the next question to examine is how they are given.

Timelessness of the Abstract Objects

In his earlier work, up to at least 1918, Husserl characterized the mode of being of the abstract objects as timeless, *überzeitlich*. For example, in *Ideas I*, Husserl distinguishes between concepts and essences to distinguish between constructed

---

[26] See also *Ideas I*, §§136–138.

[27] Zahavi recaps "constitution" "as a process that allows for manifestation and signification, that is, it must be understood as a process that permits that which is constituted to appear, unfold, articulate, and show itself as what it is" (2003, p. 73).

concepts, presentations of, say, numbers, and the numbers themselves, the time-less pure numbers (§22). In the lectures on logic and general theory of science held in 1918, Husserl is even clearer (1996, pp. 32–34, 2019, pp. 33–35):

> There are infinitely many possible empirical sets that we can count: cardinal numbers of horses, of carrots, etc. But these empirical cardinal numbers come into being and pass away, start and stop, etc. That does not, however, affect the pure cardinal numbers. If no concrete cardinal number n were to exist in the real world from a certain point in time on, then the pure number series would not for that reason have a hole between $n - 1$ and $n + 1$. (Husserl 1996, p. 32, 2019, p. 33)

Husserl accordingly claims that it is an indubitable truth that $2 < 3$ and that in the cardinal number series, 2 has its place between 1 and 3 etc. "Consequently there are objects of insightful givenness that are not things and not existential moments in the spatiotemporal world" (1996, p. 33, 2019, p. 34). They are ideal objects, but to be sure, not in the sense of being conceived in some mysterious intellectual intuition. Husserl explains:

> I embrace ideal objects for the same mundane reason that I embrace things, just because I see them, looking at them grasp them myself. I even maintain that ideal objects are in no way anything especially lofty that one could flaunt, but what is the very most ordinary, just like ordinary stones on the road. All people know them in a certain naïve way since they indeed talk of numbers and sounds and so on in ideal ways. Only philosophers do not wish to know them. They dismiss them, calling them Platonic Ideas. Granted, I say. In fact, if one recognizes givens like the series of natural numbers, or like the sequence of the sound species, as objectivities, one cannot at all describe them in any other way than with the words that Plato used to describe them in his theory of Ideas: as eternal, selfsame, as non-temporal and non-spatial, as unmoved, as unchangeable, and so on. But, instantly, Platonic Ideas – nothing but hypostatizations of abstractions – goes buzzing through the heads of those trained in traditional philosophy. (Husserl 1996, p. 34, 2019, p. 35)

Husserl thus ascribes to numbers a platonist being, but in an "ordinary sense" without hypostatization of them. They are not substantial objects that could be found in some specific Platonic realm. Instead, they exist in structures that define the objects about which they are, as seen earlier in Husserl's discussion of structuralism.

Constitution of Abstract Objects in *Formal and Transcendental Logic*

Husserl's view of the givenness of the ideal objects changes in the 1920s when he takes the generative, that is, the historical and social aspects, into consideration. While his earlier view was that the ideal objects are timeless and eternal, he now holds that they exist for us all the time "since their first constitution," as we will soon see.

In *Formal and Transcendental Logic* (1929), Husserl discusses the constitution of ideal objects in the context of the metaphysical presuppositions of the mathematicians. All objects, whether physical (real in Husserlian) or abstract (ideal in Husserlian) are given as themselves in evidence. Indeed, Husserl defines evidence as "that performance on the part of intentionality which consists in the giving of something-itself [*die intentionale Leistung der Selbstgebung*]" (1974, 1969, §59). The primitive form of it is perception, and, as before, he holds that the abstract objects are given in a manner that is in many ways analogous to perception. As in perception, "[t]he identity and, therefore, the objectness [*Gegenständlichkeit*] of something ideal can be directly 'seen'" (1974, 1969, §58). To be sure, the evidence with which both empirical and abstract objects are given is fallible, yet it is of "something-itself," as opposed to a mere picture or some other empty intention of it (such as through a mere sign) (§§58–59). Yet, abstract objects are not individuated in time, because in their case, explicit recollection turns into perception (§59). In other words, if we recollect a proof, and do so explicitly, the proof itself is given to us. But if we remember putting keys on a kitchen table, and even if the memory is very explicit, one cannot equate the memory with the perception of the keys on the kitchen table. Despite this difference, in both cases the evidence of something itself can ground the correctness of something meant (§59). Furthermore, the objects are never given individually, but in the context of all unified conscious life. The evidence is thus related to the whole life of consciousness (§59).

The objects of different categories are given in different kinds of evidence. Hence, Husserl writes, "a great *task* arises, the task of exploring all these modes of the evidence in which the objectivity intended to *shows itself*" (1974, 1969, §60, italic in the original). At this point Husserl reminds us that to think that evidence is something apodictic and absolutely indubitable, and, so to speak, absolutely finished in itself "is to bar oneself from an understanding of any scientific production" (§60). Scientific investigation in Husserl's view is self-critical and it never ceases to question itself. Our experiences typically give objects themselves only imperfectly. The abstract objects are given, "according to their various strata" likewise with legitimizing, or grounding evidence that gives something in itself. (§61)

Husserl further explains that each experience of an ideal object gives something that is numerically the same, namely, the object, which thus can be experienced many times. The objects confront us as something transcendent, external to our consciousness, because they have an identity that surpasses any single experience of them (1974, 1969, §§60–62). These objects are given as an indeterminate "itself-given identical pole" (when applied to abstract objects I suppose this would be the case with the completely indeterminate structuralist objects, as discussed earlier), "which subsequently displays itself, in 'its' (likewise ideally identical) 'determinations,' throughout the giving of its-itself, a giving that can be continued in the synthetic form: 'explication'" (§61). Husserl thus suggests that these indeterminate somethings can be further determined "according to their various strata," presumably first with grammatical determination, then what I have referred to as "contentual determination" and eventually as "material determination," which is to say that they fall under a certain essence. Experience is thus *"the primal instituting of the being-for-us of objects as having their objective sense. . ..*. Everywhere, and therefore even in the case of external experience, it is true that an evidential giving of something itself must be characterized as a process of constitution, a process whereby the object of experience arises" (§61, italic in the original).

In §63, Husserl further discusses the givenness of the abstract objects that are constituted in judging. New judgments are actively formed out of the judgments that are already given:

> As in every other acting the ends of our action, the new judgments to be produced, are consciously intended to by us beforehand in modes of an anticipation which is empty, still undetermined in respect of content, or in any case still unfulfilled; we are conscious of them thus as the things toward which we are striving and the bringing of which to an actualizing givenness of them-themselves makes up the action, as accomplished step by step. (1974, 1969, §63)

Abstract objects are constructed actively, on the basis of already given ones. Husserl sums up the constitution of the abstract objects as follows:

> *This manner of givenness – givenness as something coming from such original activity –* is nothing other than *the sort of "perception" proper to them.* Or what is the same thing, this originally acquiring activity is *the "evidence" appropriate to these idealities.* Evidence, quite universally, is indeed nothing other than the mode of consciousness – built up, perhaps, as an extraordinarily complex hierarchical structure – that offers its intentional objectivity in the mode belonging to the original "it itself." This evident-making activity of consciousness – in the present case a spontaneous activity hard to explore – is the "original constitution," stated more pregnantly, the primally institutive constitution, of ideal objectivities of the sort with which logic is concerned. (1974, 1969, §63, italic in the original)

Husserl then goes on to describe the hierarchical mapping of different kinds of evidence. First he points out that reality has precedence over every irreality, because all irrealities relate back to an actual or possible reality (§64). Hence, the paradigmatic judgment is that of a perceived physical thing.

In §73, Husserl continues to describe the evidence with which the ideal objects are given. He writes that even in the evidence of distinctness, the judgment is given as self-same, as something to which we can always return, and thus as objects "*existing for us at all times*, available to us at all times, as convictions lasting for us from the time of their first constitution" (§73, italic in the original). One can use the results as the basis for the new ones, connected to other results and so forth. Their being remains fixed as identical. Obviously, occasional shiftings can, but should not, take place. "If someone who is proving something recurs, in the proof-complex, to an earlier judgment, it must indeed be actually the same judgment" (§73). The ideal being has a transcendence in transcending the current living evidence in which it is given. Thus, the transcendence of the ideal beings is presupposed in logic as an ideal, as a norm. Curiously Husserl points out that if the intersubjectivity of the verbal expression is taken into account, the problem of constitution will be even more complex (§73).[28]

Ultimately, the evidence of clarity is gained from perceiving individuals (1974, 1969, §83). In Husserl's hierarchy of evidence the most original evidence is accrued in individual judgments, and in particular experiential judgment with a relation to a perceived individual and its determinations. The transitional link, that is, the judgment theory (mechanically) reducible to the elementary judgments, shows how to pass on evidence to the more complex judgments, and this holds separately for both distinctness and clarity. So, within the realm of distinctness, the evidence given by the distinct elementary judgments is to be sought out. Then further, in applied mathematics and logic in the realm of clarity, that is "material evidence," the same is true of the judgments about the data of possible perception and memory (§§84).

In sum, there are many kinds of dependencies in this hierarchical web of evidence: while the complex expressions are reducible to the simpler ones, truth logic derives its evidence from judgments about perceived objects and the realm of non-contradiction derives distinct evidence from the judgment-senses. The step from the realm of one kind of evidence to the other appears to involve abstraction of some kind. Hence, for Husserl, even formal mathematics has an implicit reference to the empirical reality, even though it is not reducible to it. Or, the other way around, looking at the procedure bottom-up, the formal

---

[28] Husserl writes that "[t]he problem of constitution is again broadened when we recall that verbal expression, which we excluded from our considerations of logic, is an essential presupposition for intersubjective thinking and for an intersubjectivity of the theory accepted as ideally existing; and that accordingly an ideal identifiability of the expression, as expression, must likewise raise a problem of constitution" (1974, 1969, §73).

theories are both constructed and abstracted from the judgments about perceived objects.

The abstract objects are not eternal because they have existence only after they have first been established. Yet they are given as transcendent and omnitemporal. How are we supposed to understand this as a coherent view? In the next section, in 3.2.3, I will analyze them as transcendent, but in fact as socially constructed objects, grounded in a multitude of different kinds and levels of evidence. That is, within the practice the mathematical truths appear eternal, but when looked at from a more general, historical point of view, it is in fact just so that they are available only after they have been established.

Need for Further Kinds of Evidence

Husserl's discussion implies that even further kinds of evidence should be distinguished. For example, consider formal mathematics guided by the evidence of distinctness. Since Husserl held that not all theories need to be categorical or else explicated with normalizing judgment theory, it seems that he should admit a kind of evidence of distinctness that derives from model existence. Hilbert used the idea of model existence around the turn of the century when he showed different kinds of geometries to be non-contradictory by constructing models for them, and it does not seem to be a stretch to think that Husserl acknowledges such a procedure as well. But if a theory is contentually definite but not yet empirically verified, should this not yield yet another kind of evidence of distinctness? Should not there be "transitional" evidence between distinctness and clarity? So the question arises as to whether one should carry transcendental investigation further and also identify other kinds of evidence. In lecture notes from 1927 Husserl himself wondered whether there could be two different ideas of exactness, which could serve as norms for the same empirical intuitions (Husserl 2012, p. 255). What then are the kinds of evidence related to these? In general, the transcendental phenomenological investigation should proceed to identify all the different kinds of evidence, intrinsic and extrinsic, at play in mathematics.

3 A Phenomenological Philosophy of Mathematics

The previous section already indicated what a phenomenological point of view to contemporary problems might be. A concern related to this is with what right do I call a view "phenomenological"? This section will start with an attempt to characterize the "phenomenological" philosophy of mathematics, first by focusing on how it should be conceived of with respect to Husserl's writings, and then by comparing it to other contemporary approaches. Only a programmatic description of it can be given here.

3.1 Phenomenology vs. Husserl

The main way of developing phenomenological philosophy of mathematical practice is by adopting Husserl's methodological insights and applying them in the contemporary setting. In other words, one should take the method as detailed in Section 1 and then examine mathematics as it is practiced today. This means bringing the view up to date regarding various metalogical results. In general, it implies taking into account how mathematics has evolved and fragmented into further sub-disciplines with different kinds of more specified goals and epistemic values than those that Husserl discussed and identified. A *Besinnung* of contemporary mathematics brings about a much finer map of goals and values, where some values are shared by all, whereas others can be used to differentiate and distinguish some enterprises from others. Computability is still a goal, not least thanks to the use of computers in mathematics. The development has generated a new goal in terms of complexity of computations. Categoricity is still an ideal for many since categorical axiomatizations capture uniquely particular structures (such as $\mathbb{N}$ and $\mathbb{R}$) and thus gives a reference to much of the mathematicians' informal talk. It has also developed into further species, like internal categoricity, to be briefly discussed next, and categoricity in power.[29] Entirely new kinds of evidence have surfaced. For example, thanks to the possibility of using computers in mathematics, probabilistic notions, such as the "likelihood" of whether a statement is true, have entered mathematics (see, for example, Avigad 2009, pp. 308–312).

3.1.1 On the Possible Usefulness of Husserl's Results

Since contemporary mathematics is not what it was a hundred years ago when Husserl wrote about it, it might be advisable for the phenomenologist of mathematics not to spend too much time in trying to understand Husserl's obscure unpublished notes about scientific disciplines written more than a hundred years ago. While that may be prudent to some extent, it is important not to entirely neglect his results. Many of Husserl's results are still relevant, and others may still turn out to be relevant. For example, Husserl's analyses of categoricity and computability as goals that drive mathematics characterize also the later genesis of contemporary mathematical practice. These two goals shaped the debate about the foundations of mathematics after the turn of the century. They can be found in the output of Husserl's immediate surroundings: Zermelo developed the iterative

---

[29] T is categorical or monomorphic or univalent if it has exactly one model (up to isomorphism). T is categorical in power κ if it has exactly one model in cardinality κ. These definitions are from Baldwin (2018, 49).

conception of sets in 1930 with the goal of investigating the categoricity of set theory (1930). At around the same time, not only the intuitionists, but, for example, Carnap also developed constructive, that is, what he even called "definite" language I in his *Logische Syntax der Sprache* (1934). Definiteness to him referred to the limitation of the language to those properties of numbers, "of which the possession or non-possession by any number whatsoever can be determined in a finite number of steps according to a fixed method" (Carnap 1934, 1936, §3). Hermann Weyl very aptly called the intermingling of the constructive and axiomatic styles in mathematical thinking a "dexterous blending," writing that *"large parts of modern mathematical research are based on a dexterous blending of constructive and axiomatic procedures"* (Weyl 1985, p. 38, italic in the original). These two different styles determine the present situation as Ferreirós and Grey summarize it: "The divergence of two mathematical styles, constructive and postulational, started around 1870, consolidated in the 1920s, and has continued to the present date … " (2006, 7).

Despite the recent development of internal categoricity results[30] (e.g., by Väänänen, who has shown that it can be proved in the first order; for this and a philosophically informed survey, or should say, sense-investigation of the topic, see Maddy and Väänänen 2023), and how Button and Walsh (2018) seem to think it counters modelism (the view I ascribed to Husserl in Section 2.1), the importance of categoricity results has not disappeared from mathematical practice.[31] The transcendental investigation of the practice, however, reveals a presupposition of many mathematicians for the determinacy of reference, that, for example, the natural number structure ought to be determinate. This is a similar transcendental presupposition that already Husserl identified, namely, the presupposition of the identity of abstract objects (see discussion earlier, esp. Section 2.2.2 on constitution of abstract objects in *Formal and Transcendental Logic*). Another revealed presupposition is the determinacy of truth-value, that is, the conviction that mathematical statements are in the end either true or false.[32]

As the previous paragraph shows, the Husserlian philosopher of mathematical practice does not need to start from scratch in their attempt at giving

---

[30] For the history of the term "internal categoricity," see Maddy & Väänänen (2023, pp. 6, 24–26); the term was first used in 2002, but the idea has been around since the 1990s. Internal categoricity is "internal" because it does not use any semantic notions. See also Baldwin (2018, 73–74).

[31] For example, Hamkins (2024) argues for a scenario in which categoricity, implementing in a practical manner the philosophy of structuralism, plays so central role that because of it Continuum Hypothesis should be accepted as an axiom: the categoricity of hyperreal numbers can be proven from ZFC + Continuum hypothesis. This gives a rigorous, categorical, account of hyperreal field required for coherent mathematical practice.

[32] And thus Maddy and Väänänen (2023) can be seen to engage in transcendental investigation of the presuppositions of the categoricity arguments in their revelation of what they call "pre-theoretic metaphysics." See note 33.

a phenomenology of mathematical practice. Husserl's view of *Besinnung* is natural enough to be already at work in many contemporary conceptualizations of mathematical practice. This is the case for example with Penelope Maddy's naturalism to be discussed more closely in Section 3.2.2. Stella Moon (2023) has studied homotopy type theory explicitly from the phenomenological point of view and argues that it has autonomy and rigor as its motivational goals. Baldwin's *Model Theory and Mathematical Practice* (2018) develops an entire network of properties guiding the model-theoretical practice. Baldwin describes the present-day model theoretical practice as being focused on various properties of theories to partition all theories by a family of properties as opposed to the previous paradigm in the 1950s that was focused on the study of logics and their properties. He writes: "After the paradigm shift there is a systematic search for a finite set of syntactic conditions which divide first order theories into disjoint classes such that models of different theories in the same class have similar mathematical properties. In this framework one can compare different areas of mathematics by checking where theories formalizing them lie in the classification" (2018, p. 2). This project resembles Husserl's view of the theory of theories as the science which

> deals *a priori* with the *essential sorts (forms) of theories and the relevant laws of relation [Beziehungsgesetzen]*. The idea therefore arises, all of this being taken together, of a more comprehensive science of theory in general. In its fundamental part, the essential concepts and laws which pertain constitutively to the Idea of Theory will be investigated. It will then go over to differentiating this Idea, and investigating possible theories in a priori fashion, rather than the possibility of theory in general. (1975, 2001a, §69, italic in the original)

Instead, of attempting at constructing one metatheory for various mathematical theories, Husserl suggests a framework in which to compare separate theories in terms of their properties. Similarly, Baldwin argues for local formalization: "We argue that comparing (usually first order) formalizations of different mathematical topics is a better tool for investigating the connections between their methods and results than a common coding of them into set theory" (Baldwin 2018, p. 2). In both enterprises, the formalization is local, rather than global, the aim is a systematic comparison of local formalizations for distinct mathematical areas, and the choice of vocabulary and logic appropriate to the particular topic are crucial (for Husserl on this, see Hartimo 2019). Baldwin then discusses "virtuous properties," such as categoricity in power, that provide a method for organization of theories "that has powerful consequences for finding invariants for models" (2018, 29). Virtuous properties are ones that have significant mathematical consequences for any theory holding the property (Baldwin 2018, p. 59). This means that while categoricity is not very virtuous for first-order theories, categoricity in power is a highly virtuous property of a theory. To cut a long story short, this project of classifying theories in terms of their desired properties sounds very much like Husserl's project of the theory of theories with various formulations of definiteness as the desired properties in question. All this demonstrates that the first step in developing the phenomenological philosophy of mathematical practice consists in finding already existing conceptualizations that are based on something like natural *Besinnung* and in which the existing practices are viewed in terms of their motivational goals.

Button and Walsh's (2018) argument against modelism helps bring about something important about the phenomenological point of view on mathematical practice. Button and Walsh argue that modelism presupposes too strong a background theory.[33] From the Husserlian point of view, however, this does not seem to be a problem: Husserl held that the aspiration for the Euclidean ideal, or more precisely, categoricity, as we saw earlier, has characterized the practice of mathematics implicitly since Euclid. He thought that the isomorphism types are normative ideals and such ideals need not even be reachable to be able to guide the development. It is true that in clarifying and fulfilling this intention a considerable amount of mathematics is needed. What this shows is that this task requires engaging in mathematical practice, which today presupposes a certain expertise from the practitioners. Mathematical practice is an intersubjective and intergenerational practice of experts with a certain kind of education and with a more or less passive mathematical background knowledge. Hence, for a practicing mathematician, the needed amount of background theory is not a problem for pinning down isomorphism types, such as

---

[33] Button and Walsh hold that the problem with modelism lies in its assumption of a strong background theory: to pin down an isomorphism type, the isomorphism type has to be described in some way. While this description cannot be carried out in first-order logic, nor in any logic with a finitary deductive system, it cannot be done in stronger logics either because the description carried out in stronger logics presupposes concepts that are just as mathematical as the natural number structure itself (Button & Walsh 2018, pp. 151–167). In other words, first-order logic allows for infinitely many interpretations and hence in it the number structure cannot be characterized uniquely (i.e., categorically, up to isomorphism). The second-order characterization is categorical in standard interpretation, but it can also be given a Henkin model so that categoricity fails. Choosing among these models requires grasping second-order notions, and hence a relatively complicated background theory. The argument is originally made by Putnam 1980, p. 481. Button and Walsh view this as an argument to prefer the syntactical notion of internal categoricity. Maddy and Väänänen 2023 take Button and Walsh as well as Parsons to have objectionable pre-theoretic metaphysics in seeking for determinateness, in Parsons' case for our concept of natural numbers and in case of Button and Walsh, determinacy of the truth-value for CH (2023, p. 50). See also Baldwin (2018, 73–74) for an argument why internal categoricity does not specify reference for the second order sentence Φ; it merely shows that the sentence refers to a unique isomorphism type but does not identify that type or its theory.

the natural numbers. It rather shows the amount of enculturation needed to characterize such structures.[34]

In conclusion, Husserl's results can be taken as pointers for seeing more clearly how to apply the method (hence the importance of Section 2). It shows that *Besinnung* of the mathematicians' practice is a rather down-to-earth attempt to conceptualize what the mathematicians are really doing in terms of their aims and the historical *Besinnung* helps to put this practice into its historical context. Obviously, the phenomenological philosophy of mathematics should not restrict itself to the state that mathematics was in at Husserl's time. But Husserl's results show something about the genesis of contemporary conceptualizations and thus they help to isolate different contemporary styles of doing mathematics. Many existing accounts of mathematical practice come close to Husserl's natural *Besinnung* and can thus be taken as a starting point for the phenomenological reflection. The more enduring and more unique results of the phenomenological method, however, are the revealed transcendental conditions of possibility, to be discussed next.

3.1.2 Judgment Theoretical Construction and Transcendental Clarification as Studies of the Intensionality of Mathematics

The way in which mathematical acts and their objects are given to us is, in the present-day philosophy of mathematics, referred to as the question about the intensionality (with an *s*) of mathematics. For example, in a recent publication, Antonutti Marfori and Quinon write that "[i]ntensionality in mathematics is [...] traditionally understood as concerning the way in which mathematical objects are presented to us, and how the way in which we represent those objects affects what we can know about them" (2021, p. 996). While these authors do not have the phenomenological point of view in mind, their characterization fits the description of the task of the transcendental phenomenology of mathematics perfectly, that is, how are mathematical acts and their objects given to us? Solomon Feferman has claimed that intensionality in mathematics is neglected because of the prevalent set-theoretical view of mathematics: "Intensionality in mathematics has to do with how mathematical objects are presented to us. Intensional considerations are given short shrift in the current dominant platonistic, extensional view of mathematics. According to that view, mathematical

---

[34] This is also something one could learn from Matthieu Queloz's account of pragmatic genealogy: the concepts cannot be discussed in isolation: "Ideas are in their element in distinctive contexts of purposive human action, action that takes place against a background of contingent facts about us and the world we live in. Trying to understand the ideas we live by in isolation from the circumstances in which they are felicitously deployed is like studying a shoal of beached fish as if they were in their natural habitat" (2021, p. 1).

objects have an existence which is independent of us and of any means of definition and construction" (1985, p. 41). This raises two issues: first, to the phenomenologist the problem of givenness concerns all extant mathematics, and hence it concerns both the platonistic and the constructivistic aspects of mathematics. To be sure, these two styles are not given in a similar way, but they are characterized by different kinds of evidence as norms guiding them. Feferman, however, in restricting the problem of givenness to the construct-ivist style thereby expresses philosophy-first statements about platonism in mathematics.

The second issue is the distinction between the natural and the transcen-dental points of view. The judgment-theoretical construction takes place in the natural attitude. In Husserl's view all acts carried out in mathematics are carried out in a theory of judgments, in a natural (critical) attitude. These acts include collecting, counting, ordering, combining, and transforming (Husserl 1969, §39, 2019, §22). Contemporary philosophy of mathematical practices teaches us that to be exhaustive the theory of judgments should be expanded to include also acts of drawing diagrams and pictures, the usage of computers, and so forth. Generally, one could think of classification of differ-ent ways of constructing mathematical theories in terms how permissive the theory of judgment in question is and how the acts of construction relate to different areas of mathematics as specified earlier and by taking into account the metalogical results acquired since Husserl's days. For Husserl the theory of judgments is governed by a norm of grammatical correctness. One question to address in the contemporary context is whether the construction indeed needs to be linguistically expressible at all?

The transcendental reflection on the theory of judgments turns to reflect the process of construction itself, its goals and the kinds of evidence, as well as its presuppositions as discussed earlier. The transcendental investigation of con-temporary mathematical practice should examine for example the role of image-consciousness in mathematical proofs. I am not aware of any actual work on the topic in the context of mathematical practice, but there is an entire volume of *Husserliana* on *Phantasy, Image Consciousness, and Memory* to give some guidelines for how a phenomenologist would look at it.

Husserl's transcendental analysis eventually arrives at explicating general structures of consciousness and problems such as intersubjectivity and time-consciousness. These results are less dependent on the particular socio-historical context than the previously described results of natural sense-investigation are. For that reason, they are more stable results (nothing, of course, is conclusive in phenomenology because, as Husserl put it, it would be "unscientific" to think so; the phenomenological results are always open to reflection and questioning). As explained earlier, the transcendental examination of this practice shows that it takes place in judgments that are ultimately grounded on perception or memory of empirical objects. The objects of perception in turn are (constituted as) intersubjective objects, perceivable by anyone. They can be made the center of our attention or they may remain in the background. The awareness of where they are with respect to us brings the problem of embodiment into the picture. Sensing the distance, that is, how far they are from us, requires sensing (proprioception) in which direction our eyes are looking. The empirical objects are constituted to have horizons that make us anticipate finding in them some further aspects or some other objects typically accompanied by them. Something similar takes place among the ideal objects, where "the construction of those already known opens in advance a horizon of objects capable of being further discovered, although still unknown" as Husserl puts it in the previously cited quotation (Husserl 1985, 1973c, §64 c). This kind of horizontality presupposes the irreducibly subjective temporal me that is not shared by anyone. Here, we find our consciousness to be a stream with a primal impression of now, a forward-looking and expectant protention, and the retention of what just happened and what is sinking into the past. To this consciousness, everything in the world, including mathematics, is given. And it is the ultimate unifying source of all scientific knowledge.

3.2 The Phenomenological Philosophy of Mathematics in Comparison

Section 2 discussed the way in which the mathematicians constitute the abstract objects as transcendent to them, that is, as existing independently of us. This holds for both the structuralistic indeterminate objects as well as the more concretely given constructed objects (that we analyzed by way of intuitionistic type theory) which have contentual determinacy, but are also similarly viewed as transcendent to us, that is, they also have omnitemporal existence after their first constitution. In what follows I will characterize the phenomenological view in more detail by comparing it to a few other approaches to mathematics. I will start by situating the phenomenological point of view within the contemporary philosophy of mathematical practice.

3.2.1 Phenomenology vs. the Philosophy of Mathematical Practice: Mancosu and the Mavericks

Paolo Mancosu's introduction to *Philosophy of Mathematical Practice* (2008) summarizes the program of the philosophy of mathematical practice by looking at its genesis that combines two traditions: what he calls the "maverick" tradition, the term originally coined by Kitcher, and the development of the naturalist philosophy of mathematics within the mainstream analytic philosophy of mathematics. This latter development culminates in Penelope Maddy's work (1997, 2007, 2012), which I will discuss in the next section. Here, I want to briefly characterize Husserl's approach vis-à-vis the mavericks as a kind of orientation for how to locate phenomenology in the philosophy of mathematical practice.

The maverick tradition has its roots in Imre Lakatos's work in the 1960s; since then it has been developed by Philip Kitcher (1984) and many others in the 1980s. The authors in this tradition called for historically more faithful analysis of mathematics, wanting to answer questions such as "How does mathematics grow?" "What is mathematical progress?" What makes some mathematical ideas (or theories) better than others? What is mathematical explanation? My intention is not to give a detailed and full view of the now rather expansive literature in this tradition, but to briefly situate Husserl's view with respect to them. For that purpose, I will compare the phenomenological approach to mathematical practice to the three characteristics with which Mancosu sums up the maverick view (2008, p. 5). These three characteristics are:

1. Anti-foundationalism, that is, there is no certain foundation for mathematics; mathematics is a fallible activity.
2. Anti-logicism, that is, mathematical logic cannot provide the tools for an adequate analysis of mathematics – in particular the dynamics of mathematical discovery and its historical development.
3. Attention to mathematical practice: only detailed analysis and reconstruction of large and significant parts of mathematical practice can provide a philosophy of mathematics worth its name.

The phenomenological philosophy of mathematical practice is similarly anti-foundationalist: Husserl is not in the quest to give certain foundations to mathematics. Mathematics for him is a fallible activity. Husserl held that to think that evidence is something apodictic and absolutely indubitable, and, so to speak, absolutely finished in itself, "is to bar oneself from an understanding of any scientific production" (1974, 1969, §60). Such a foundationalist view is not productive for the scientific attitude, which is intrinsically and eternally self-critical in Husserl's view. Husserl can be viewed to offer "descriptive" foundations, or "Socratic" foundations, but this kind of foundationalism does not contradict the anti-foundationalism of the philosophers of mathematical practice. The topic is admittedly rather complex and merits a more detailed discussion on another occasion.

The issue with mathematical logic is not quite as straightforward as it is according to Mancosu's characterization of the mavericks. Mathematical logic obviously does not provide an adequate analysis of mathematics and its development, and hence the phenomenologist agrees with the mavericks. The phenomenologists demand a genealogical examination of the development of mathematics conceived as social practice and then an examination of its conditions of possibility. However, as discussed in the previous section the employment of formal methods can be useful, and a kind of local formalization appears to be in line with Husserl's vision of theory of theories. Yet, there are formal methods that instead seem to cover up the nuances at stake, and the phenomenologist should worry about such a possibility as well. In sum, while formal methods are not sufficient for the analysis of mathematical practice, they may turn out to be useful for the project. However, this does not make Husserl a logicist by any means. Indeed, the phenomenologist's point of view is closer to naturalism in mathematics than logicism.

This brings us to the last of Mancosu's characteristics: to attention to mathematical practice. Husserl started to include socio-historical aspects in his phenomenological analyses in the 1920s. He was led to them by examining the presuppositions of the formal theories. Mathematical theories presuppose that they are constructed in intersubjective practices by conscious human beings who live in the world, as explained earlier repeatedly (see also Hartimo & Rytilä 2023). On this score, the phenomenological philosophy of mathematics obviously agrees with the views of the maverick tradition.

3.2.2 Phenomenological Philosophy of Mathematics vs. Second Philosophy

Apart from the mavericks, Mancosu analyzes the philosophy of mathematical practice as having another genealogy within analytic philosophy. Here, the philosophy of mathematical practice grows out of Quine's naturalism, finding its most representative expression in Penelope Maddy's mathematical naturalism, which I will discuss next.

To begin, let us note that Penelope Maddy characterizes the fundamental spirit of all naturalism as

> the conviction that a successful enterprise, be it science or mathematics, should be understood and evaluated on its own terms, that such an enterprise should not be subject to criticism from, and does not stand in need of support from, some external, supposedly higher point of view. (Maddy 1997, p. 185)

Note that, according to this description of naturalism, fundamental to it is what has been referred to earlier with the slogan "back to the things themselves." Phenomenology primarily wants to account for mathematics on its own terms. This aspiration should be distinguished from the use of natural scientific reductionism in *philosophy* that Husserl found problematic. In his view, philosophy should not reduce consciousness, ideas, ideals, and norms away from the studied phenomena (Husserl 1911, 1981; for a detailed discussion, see Hartimo 2020a). This is, however, not the case with Maddy's naturalism, which emphasizes the goal-directedness of the mathematicians' practices. Hence, the method of (natural) *Besinnung* comes very close to Maddy's naturalized methodology.

The naturalistic method that Maddy introduced in her *Naturalism in Mathematics* (1997) is informed by a study of historical cases that give both negative and positive counsel. The negative counsel shows that certain (typically philosophical) questions are ultimately irrelevant to the practice of mathematics. The positive counsel shows a pattern whose considerations are relevant and decisive. To do so, the method identifies the goals of the practices and evaluates whether the practice in question is an effective means toward its goal (p. 194).

This comes close to Husserl's method of sense-investigation. Like Maddy's naturalist philosopher, the Husserlian phenomenological philosopher also analyzes mathematical aims, notes whether these aims conflict or are confused, and examines whether the mathematicians are really reaching their goals. Thus, with Leng, we can claim that the phenomenological point of view on mathematics, like Maddy's naturalism, strives to understand and evaluate mathematics "on its own terms," which means abandoning "the possibility of providing a revisionary philosophy of mathematics for *purely* philosophical reasons" (Leng 2002, p. 6). The two methods diverge on the meta level: whereas Husserl turns to transcendental reflections to examine the conditions of possibility of this kind of practice, Maddy invokes the empirical Second Philosopher. Whereas phenomenological philosophy is ultimately tied to spelling out the practitioner's point of view, Maddy, from her meta-perspective, is able to philosophize irrespective of what the practitioners think they are doing. The empirical Second Philosopher obtains a somewhat reductionistic view of mathematics in contrast to most practitioners. Maddy does not sanction mathematicians' metaphysical beliefs, or skepticism about the existence of mathematical objects for that matter. Practice is all that counts, and the mathematicians' metaphysical beliefs are irrelevant for the practice itself (see especially 2012, pp. 99–112). The view is thin in the sense that it does not demand coming up with a story about the epistemology of such structures. Practice is also all that counts for that purpose. For the Second Philosopher, mathematics is a practice and only a practice, with no metaphysical implications or epistemological enigmas.

Whereas Maddy wants to be faithful to mathematical practice and mathematicians' practice-related goals, the Husserlian phenomenologist also wants to be faithful to the mathematicians' intentions, further values, and beliefs about their subject matter. As we saw earlier, the mathematicians' metaphysical beliefs work as implicit presuppositions in their practices. The phenomenologist's task is to make them explicit, to uncover the "natural" metaphysics implicit in practice as examined in Section 2.2.2. This implied metaphysics has also some social constructivist aspects to be discussed next.

3.2.3 Metaphysical Implications: Constituted Realism within Social Constructivism?

The phenomenological philosopher as described in *Formal and Transcendental Logic* uses two methods – sense-investigation, that is, *Besinnung*, and transcendental clarification, in combination – to capture the mathematicians' intentions.[35] With these methods, *Besinnung* and transcendental phenomenological reflection, the phenomenological philosopher aims at capturing the practice of mathematics "as it is," that is, metaphysically neutrally, as explained earlier. Yet, the approach has metaphysical implications for the way in which the ontology of mathematics is perceived. First, it obviously rules out naïvely idealist and realist views about mathematical objects: abstract objects of mathematics are not subjective constructions nor are they "absurd things-in-themselves" as Husserl would put it.

But what are the more positive implications? As discussed earlier, Husserl's view with regard to the mathematical objects seems to change. His view in 1918 was still that they are timeless, eternal, and unchanging entities, which suggests platonism, or more specifically non-eliminative structuralism. However, later he started to view them as "available at all times" since their first establishment. Instead of his early platonism, his later view is closer to the humanist view of mathematics as discussed by Reuben Hersh (1997). Hersh views mathematics as a historically evolved social phenomenon, intelligible only in a social context. According to him, nevertheless, "[o]nce created and communicated, mathematical objects are *there*. They detach from their originator and become part of human culture" (1997, p. 16). The change in Husserl's view from regarding abstract objects as timeless to seeing them as constructed at some point after which they are always available to us appears to be one from platonism with regard to mathematical objects to humanism. This change raises an interpretative question: is this change a move from a more realistic view to idealism regarding mathematical objects or should we consider the later position as an enrichment and specification of the earlier view? I believe the latter is the case as a correct reading of Husserl's texts and in line with Husserl's own views about the way he progressed as discussed earlier (in note 6 in particular).

In the 1920s Husserl broadened his earlier view by taking social and historical factors into account. Thus, he had to embed his earlier constituted realism

---

[35] In his writings in general, Husserl uses all kinds of other methods too, such as the method of free variation, logic, and philosophical thought-experiments (such as his discussion of Twin Earth in 1911; Husserl 1987, pp. 202–219).

about the abstract objects into a more general picture of mathematical practice as social. At this time, for example, he describes the scientific practice as a self-critical enterprise that takes place within

> a community of scientific investigators, which goes on working *ad infinitum*, a community united in respect of activities and habitualities of theoretical reason. Here we shall mention only the working of investigators for and with one another and their criticizing of one another's results, those obtained by one investigator being taken over as works that pave the way for others, and so forth. (Husserl 1974, 1969, §7)

On this view, any scientific theory, including those in mathematics, is socially constructed, as they are products of social practices. That scientific theories are socially constructed in this sense, should not be very controversial.[36] For Husserl, in particular, science, logic, and mathematics are theoretical practices that aim for objective results through self-critical social practices. The papers are peer-reviewed, and some results are shown to be mistaken while others remain as lasting acquisitions. The results are available to everyone in the mathematical community since their first establishment.

But how is this view not in tension with his earlier view that they are eternal? A passage from Husserl's published *Experience and Judgment* provides the necessary clues:

> Objectivities of the understanding make their appearance in the world (a state of affairs is "discovered") as irreal; after having been discovered, they can be thought of anew and as often as desired and, in general, can be objects of experience according to their nature. But afterwards we say: even before they were discovered, they were already "valid"; or we say that they can be assumed – provided that subjects which have the ability to produce them are present and conceivable – to be producible precisely at any time, and that they have this mode of omnipresent existence: in all possible modes of productions they would be the same. Similarly, we say: "there are" mathematical and other irreal objects which no one has yet constructed. Their existence, to be sure, is revealed only by their construction (their

---

[36] Using the term "social construction" as defined by Aaron Griffith: "for some item to be socially constructed is for it to be a product of social factors, including e.g., social practices, arrangements, conventions, and institutions. The constructed item is (causally or non-causally) derived from and dependent upon certain social factors for its existence, nature, or features; the item would not exist, or be the way it is, were it not for these factors" (Griffith 2018, 394). It is rather uncontroversial that mathematical theorems, proofs, and so on are socially constructed in this sense, as they are the results of social practices. However, the decisive question is whether mathematical truths are socially constructed. In Husserl's view the attempt is to actualize them in the self-critical practice. There is no other way to access them, other than by way of mathematical practice, which goes on ad infinitum. Whether a theorem is correct or not is not in the end constructed but we cannot find out about it in any other way than through this social, self-critical practice.

"experience"), but the construction of those already known opens in advance a horizon of objects capable of being further discovered, although still unknown. As long as they are not discovered (by anyone), they are not actually in spatiotemporality; and as long as it is possible (how far this is possible, there is no need to decide here) that they never will be discovered, it may be that they will have no world-reality. But in any case, *once* they have been actualized or "realized," they are also localized spatiotemporally, but in such a way, to be sure, that this localization does not actually individualize them. (Husserl 1985, 1973c, §64 c, italic in the original)

This passage, I believe, clarifies the situation. Consider a mathematical truth, say, that axiom of choice is independent of Zermelo-Frankel axioms of set theory. That negation of axiom of choice is not a theorem of ZF was discovered by Gödel in 1938 and that axiom of choice is not its theorem was discovered Paul Cohen in 1963. These results can be thought of anew as often as desired, as Husserl puts it, assuming that there are people around who can understand and repeat the proofs of these theorems. When Gödel and Cohen proved their results, the results were actualized, and also localized spatiotemporally (i.e., written in papers or uttered at conferences). Thus, they reveal the existence of a mathematical truth, which was not "actually in spatiotemporality" around the turn of the twentieth century. These events are historical events that have taken place in a historically developed and contingent tradition of doing mathematics. Yet we think that this truth was valid even before Gödel's and Cohen's proofs.

Mathematical truths are uncovered in social construction by members of a community of mathematicians. They are revealed in a process that is so constrained that they appear transcendent to the investigator. We think that the truth is valid even if there were no human beings around. However, in practice, Gödel and Cohen needed to bring the result into "spatiotemporality" for it to become omnipresent and available. This meant that these results underwent critical appraisal by means of the mathematical community to be fully, socially accepted entities. Thus, mathematical truths are eternally and necessarily valid from the point of view of an individual mathematician, a point of view internal to mathematics as historical and contingent cultural practice. Ultimately, Husserl in *Formal and Transcendental Logic* (1929) suggests that the truth is a limit concept revealed by scientific reason that goes on *ad infinitum* (e.g., 1974, 1969, §§7, 45). Yet, at one given time the mathematical truths are constituted as both necessary and contingent, while the latter is due to the fact that they are revealed or actualized in a contingently developing cultural practice that could have developed in some other way.

Conclusion: Unity and the Mathematical Practices

So, what kind of unity phenomenology could bring to the philosophy of mathematical practice? The phenomenologist's aim is not to acquire encyclopedic awareness of the obtained results, but to obtain unity by clarification and classification of different goals, values, and kinds of Evidenz guiding the mathematicians and showing how they relate to the subjectivity. Theodore Kisiel has aptly characterized Husserl as providing three bases for the unity of the sciences: the formal logical level of theory, pretheoretical material level of their domains in the lifeworld, and finally the transcendental level of subjectivity (1970, p. 13). This Element focused on exact sciences, and hence, the properly material domains were not discussed except in passing. The formal logical level of theory was divided into the mathematical (postulational) and the judgment theoretical attitudes. The theory of judgments in which the theories are constructed from the elementary concepts up, is, when aiming at truth, what relates the formal level to the lifeworld. The transcendental level of subjectivity demands a study of presuppositions and the kinds of Evidenz, and ultimately reveals the presupposition of the mathematician as a human being in an intersubjective lifeworld. The resulting philosophy demands an infinite task of clarification, in which the new developments are placed into the framework of goals aimed at in diverse areas of mathematics, and in which the evidential basis and the various presuppositions required for different kinds of practices are continually re-examined. The metaphysical implications of this method show how the objectivist mathematics is at the same time historically constructed and platonistically given.

References

Antonutti Marfori, M. & Quinon, P. (2021). Intensionality in Mathematics: Problems and Prospects. Special Issue on Intensionality in Mathematics. *Synthese*, 198 (5), 995–999.

Avigad, J. (2008). Computers in Mathematical Inquiry. In P. Mancosu, ed., *Philosophy of Mathematical Practice*. Oxford: Oxford University Press, pp. 302–316.

Bachelard, S. (1968). *A Study of Husserl's Formal and Transcendental Logic*, Evanston: Northwestern University Press.

Baldwin, J. T. (2018). *Model Theory and the Philosophy of Mathematical Practice: Formalization without Foundationalism*. New York: Cambridge University Press.

Beaney, M. ed. (1997). *The Frege Reader*, Oxford; Malden: Blackwell.

Becker, O. (1923). Beiträge zur phänomenologischen Begründung der Geometrie und ihrer physikalischen Anwendungen. *Jahrbuch für Philosophie und phänomenologische Forschung*, 6, 385–560.

Bernays, P. (1935). On Platonism in Mathematics. In P. Benacerraf & H. Putnam, eds., *Philosophy of Mathematics, Selected Readings, 2nd ed.* Cambridge: Cambridge University Press, pp. 258–271.

Button, T. & Walsh, S. (2018). *Philosophy and Model Theory*, Oxford: Oxford University Press.

Carnap, R. (1934). *Logische Syntax der Sprache*, Vienna: J. Springer.

Carnap, R. (1936). *Logical Syntax of Language*, Smeaton, A., transl., London: Routledge & Kegan Paul.

Carnap, R. (1950). Empiricism, Semantics, and Ontology. *Revue Internationale de Philosophie*, 4 (11), 20–40.

Carr, D. (1999). *The Paradox of Subjectivity: The Self in the Transcendental Tradition*, Oxford: Oxford University Press.

Carr, D. (2022). Phenomenology as Critical Method. In S. Aldea, D. Carr, & S. Heinämaa, eds., *Phenomenology as Critique: Why Method Matters*. New York: Routledge, pp. 9–24.

Carter, J. (2019). Philosophy of Mathematical Practice – Motivations, Themes and Prospects. *Philosophia Mathematica*, 27 (1), 1–32.

Cobb-Stevens, R. (1990). *Husserl and Analytic Philosophy*, Dordrecht: Kluwer.

Corfield, D. (2003). *Towards a Philosophy of Real Mathematics*. Cambridge: Cambridge University Press.

Corry, L. (2004). Introduction: The History of Modern Mathematics – Writing and Rewriting. *Science in Context*, 17 (1/2), 1–21.

Crosilla, L. (2022). The Entanglement of Logic and Set Theory, Constructively. *Inquiry*, 65 (6), 638–659.

Crowell, S. (2001). *Husserl, Heidegger and the Space of Meaning*, Evanston: Northwestern University Press.

Dreben, B. and Kanamori, A. (1997). Hilbert and Set Theory. *Synthese*, 110, 77–125.

Dybjer, P. & Palmgren, E. (2020). Intuitionistic Type Theory. *The Stanford Encyclopedia of Philosophy* (Summer 2020 Edition), Edward N. Zalta, ed., https://plato.stanford.edu/archives/sum2020/entries/type-theory-intuitionistic/.

Ewald, W. (1996). *From Kant to Hilbert: A Source Book in the Foundations of Mathematics*, Vol. II, Oxford: Clarendon Press.

Feferman, S. (1985). Intensionality in Mathematics. *Journal of Philosophical Logic*, 14, 41–55.

Feferman, S. (1999). Does Mathematics Need New Axioms? *American Mathematical Monthly*, 106, 99–111.

Ferreirós, J. (2016). *Mathematical Knowledge and the Interplay of Practices*, Princeton: Princeton University Press.

Ferreirós, J. & Gray, J. eds. (2006). *Architecture of Modern Mathematics: Essays in History and Philosophy*, Oxford: Oxford University Press.

Føllesdal, D. (1958). *Husserl und Frege, Ein Beitrag zur Beleuchtung der Entstehung der Phänomenologischen Philosophie*, Oslo: H. Aschehoug.

Frege, G. (1893). *Grundgesetze der Arithmetik*, Vol. I, Jena: Pohle.

Giardino, V. (2017). The Practical Turn in Philosophy of Mathematics: A Portrait of a Young Discipline. *Phenomenology and Mind*, 12, 18–28.

Gödel, K. (1961). The Modern Development of the Foundations of Mathematics in the Light of Philosophy (*1961/?). In S. Feferman, J. W. Dawson Jr., W. Goldfarb, C. Parsons, & R. N. Solovay, eds., *Kurt Gödel, Collected Works 3, Unpublished Essays and Lectures*. Oxford: Oxford University Press, pp. 374–387.

Griffith, A. M. (2018). Social Construction as Grounding. *Philosophy and Phenomenological Research*, 97 (2), 393–409.

Hamkins, J. D. (2024). How the Continuum Hypothesis Could Have Been a Fundamental Axiom. *Journal for the Philosophy of Mathematics*, arxiv: https://arxiv.org/abs/2407.02463.

Hartimo, M. (2006). Mathematical Roots of Phenomenology: Husserl and the Concept of Number. *Journal of History and Philosophy of Logic*, 27 (4), 319–337.

Hartimo, M. (2010). The Development of Mathematics and the Birth of Phenomenology. In M. Hartimo, ed., *Phenomenology and Mathematics*. Dordrecht: Springer, pp. 107–121.

Hartimo, M. (2017a). Husserl and Hilbert. In S. Centrone, ed., *Essays on Husserl's Logic and Philosophy of Mathematics*. Dordrecht: Springer, pp. 245–263.

Hartimo, M. (2017b). Husserl and Gödel's Incompleteness Theorems. *The Review of Symbolic Logic*, 10 (4), 638–650.

Hartimo, M. (2018). Radical Besinnung in Formale und transzendentale Logik (1929). *Husserl Studies*, 34, 247–266.

Hartimo, M. (2019). Husserl on Kant, and the Critical View of Logic. *Inquiry: An Interdisciplinary Journal of Philosophy*, 65 (6), 707–724.

Hartimo, M. (2020a). Husserl's Transcendentalization of Mathematical Naturalism. *Journal of Transcendental Philosophy*, 1 (3), 289–306.

Hartimo, M. (2020b). Husserl on "*Besinnung*" and Formal Ontology. In F. Kjosavik & C. Serck-Hanssen, eds., *Metametaphysics and the Sciences: Historical and Philosophical Perspectives*. New York: Routledge, pp. 200–215.

Hartimo, M. (2021a). *Husserl and Mathematics*, Cambridge: Cambridge University Press.

Hartimo, M. (2021b). *Formal and Transcendental Logic* – Husserl's Most Mature Reflection on Mathematics and Logic. In H. Jacobs, ed., *The Husserlian Mind*. London: Routledge, pp. 50–59.

Hartimo, M. (2021c). The Chimera of Logicism: Husserl's Criticism of Frege. In F. Boccuni & A. Sereni, eds., *Origins and Varieties of Logicism: A Foundational Journey in the Philosophy of Mathematics*. New York: Routledge, pp. 197–214.

Hartimo, M. (2022a). Epistemic Values and Their Phenomenological Critique. In S. Heinämaa, M. Hartimo, & I. Hirvonen, eds., *Contemporary Phenomenologies of Normativity: Norms, Goals, and Values*. New York: Routledge, pp. 234–251.

Hartimo, M. (2022b). Radical Besinnung as a Method for Critique. In A. Aldea, D. Carr, & S. Heinämaa, eds., *Phenomenology as Critique: Why Method Matters*. New York: Routledge, pp. 80–94.

Hartimo, M. & Okada, M. (2018). Syntactic Reduction in Husserl's Early Phenomenology of Arithmetic. *Synthese*, 193 (3), 937–969. https://doi.org/10.1007/s11229-015-0779-0.

Hartimo, M. & Rytilä, J. (2023). No Magic: From Phenomenology of Practice to Social Ontology of Mathematics. *Topoi*, 42, 283–295. https://doi.org/10.1007/s11245-022-09859-1.

Heinämaa, S., Hartimo, M., & Hirvonen, I. (2022). Introduction: Phenomenological Approaches to Normativity. In S. Heinämaa, M. Hartimo, & I. Hirvonen, eds., *Contemporary Phenomenologies of Normativity: Norms, Goals, and Values*. New York: Routledge, pp. 1–16.

Hersh, R. (1997). *What Is Mathematics, Really?* New York: Oxford University Press.

Hilbert, D. (1996). Die logischen Grundlagen der Mathematik. *Mathematische Annalen*, 88, 151–165.

Hilbert, D. (1922). Logical Foundations of Mathematics. Lecture Given at the Deutsche Naturforscher-Gesellschaft, September 1922. In W. B. Ewald, transl., and ed., *From Kant to Hilbert, a Source Book in the Foundations of Mathematics*. Oxford: Clarendon Press, pp. 1134–1148.

Hill, C. O. (2019). Translator's Introduction. In E. Husserl, ed., *Logic and General Theory of Science Lectures 1917/18, with Supplementary Texts from the First Version of 1910/11*. Cham: Springer, pp. XXIII–L.

Hill, C. O. & Rosado Haddock, G. (2000). *Husserl or Frege? Meaning, Objectivity, and Mathematics*, Chicago: Open Court.

Hirvonen, I. (2022). Reconciling the Noema Debate. *Axiomathes*, 32 (Suppl 3), 901–929. https://doi.org/10.1007/s10516-022-09643-1.

Husserl, E. (1911). Philosophie als strenge Wissenschaft. *Logos*, 1, 289–341.

Husserl, E. (1969). *Formal and Transcendental Logic*, Cairns, D., transl., The Hague: Martinus Nijhoff.

Husserl, E. (1970a). *Philosophie der Arithmetik*, Eley, L., ed., Husserliana XII, The Hague: Martinus Nijhoff.

Husserl, E. (1970b). *The Crisis of European Sciences and Transcendental Phenomenology, an Introduction to Phenomenological Philosophy*, Carr, D., transl., Evanston: Northwestern University Press.

Husserl, E. (1973a). *Cartesianische Meditationen und Pariser Vorträge*, Strasser, S., ed., Husserliana I, The Hague: Martinus Nijhoff.

Husserl, E. (1973b). *Zur Phänomenologie der Intersubjektivität. Texte aus dem Nachlaß. Erster Teil: 1905–1920*, Kern, I., ed., Husserliana XIII, The Hague: Martinus Nijhoff.

Husserl, E. (1973c). *Experience and Judgment: Investigations in a Genealogy of Logic*, Landgrebe, L., ed., Churchill, J. S. Churchill & Ameriks, K., transl., Evanston: Northwestern University Press.

Husserl, E. (1974). *Formale und transzendentale Logik: Versuch einer Kritik der logischen Vernunft*, Janssen, P., ed., Husserliana XVII, The Hague: Martinus Nijhoff.

Husserl, E. (1975). *Prolegomena zur reinen Logik*, Holenstein, E., ed., Husserliana XVIII, The Hague: Martinus Nijhoff.

Husserl, E. (1976a). *Ideen zu einer reinen Phänomenologie und phänomenologischen Philosophie. Erstes Buch: Allgemeine Einführung in die reine Phänomenologie,* Schuhmann, K., ed., Husserliana III/1, The Hague: Martinus Nijhoff.

Husserl, E. (1976b). *Die Krisis der europäischen Wissenschaften und die transzendentale Phänomenologie,* Biemel, W., ed., Husserliana VI, The Hague: Martinus Nijhoff.

Husserl, E. (1981). Philosophy as Rigorous Science. In Q. Lauer, transl., P. McCormick & F. A. Elliston, eds., *Husserl, Shorter Works.* South Bend: University of Notre Dame Press, pp. 166–197.

Husserl, E. (1984). *Logische Untersuchungen. Zweiter Band, Erster Teil. Untersuchungen zur Phänomenologie und Theorie der Erkenntnis,* Panzer, U., ed., Husserliana XIX/I, The Hague: Martinus Nijhoff.

Husserl, E. (1985). *Erfahrung und Urteil: Untersuchungen zur Genealogie der Logik, 6th ed.,* Landgrebe, L., ed., Hamburg: Felix Meiner Verlag.

Husserl, E. (1987). *Vorlesungen über Bedeutungslehre Sommersemester* 1908, Panzer, U., ed., Husserliana XXVI, The Hague: Martinus Nijhoff.

Husserl, E. (1996). *Logik und allgemeine Wissenschaftstheorie: Vorlesungen 1917/18,* Panzer, U., ed., Husserliana XXX, Dordrecht: Kluwer.

Husserl, E. (1999). *Cartesian Meditations: An Introduction to Phenomenology,* Cairns, D., transl., Dordrecht: Kluwer.

Husserl, E. (2001a). *Logical Investigations,* Vol. I, Findlay, J. N., transl., London: Routledge.

Husserl, E. (2001b). *Logical Investigations,* Vol. II, Findlay, J. N., transl., London: Routledge.

Husserl, E. (2001c). *Natur und Geist: Vorlesungen Sommersemester 1927,* Weiler, M., ed., Husserliana XXXII. Dordrecht: Kluwer.

Husserl, E. (2001d). Husserls Manuskripte zu seinem Göttinger Doppelvortrag von 1901. *Husserl Studies,* 17, 87–123.

Husserl, E. (2003). *Philosophy of Arithmetic: Psychological and Logical Investigations with Supplementary Texts from 1887-1901,* Willard, D., transl., Dordrecht: Kluwer Academic Publishers.

Husserl, E. (2012). *Zur Lehre vom Wesen und zur Methode der Eidetischen Variation: Texte aus dem Nachlass 1891–1935,* Fonfara, D., ed., Husserliana XLI. Dordrecht: Springer.

Husserl, E. (2014). *Ideas for a Pure Phenomenology and Phenomenological Philosophy. First Book: General Introduction to Pure Phenomenology,* Dahlstrom, D. O., transl., Indianapolis: Hackett.

Husserl, E. (2019). *Logic and General Theory of Science,* Hill, C. O., transl., Cham: Springer.

Iemhoff, R. (2020). Intuitionism in the Philosophy of Mathematics. *The Stanford Encyclopedia of Philosophy* (Fall 2020 Edition), Edward N. Zalta, ed., https://plato.stanford.edu/archives/fall2020/entries/intuitionism/.

Kant, I. (1998). *Critique of Pure Reason*, Guyer, P. & Wood, A. W. transl. and eds., Cambridge: Cambridge University Press.

Kisiel, T. (1970). Phenomenology as the Science of Science. In J. Kockelmans & T. Kisiel, eds., *Phenomenology and the Natural Sciences*. Evanston: Northwestern University Press, pp. 5–44.

Kitcher, P. (1984). *The Nature of Mathematical Knowledge*. Oxford: Oxford University Press.

Klev, A. (2017). Husserl's Logical Grammar. *History and Philosophy of Logic*, 39 (3), 232–269.

Kouri Kissel, T. & Shapiro, S. (2020). Logical Pluralism and Normativity. *Inquiry*, 63 (3–4), 389–410.

Leng, M. (2002). Phenomenology and Mathematical Practice. *Philosophia Mathematica*, 10 (3), 3–25.

Ierna, C. & Lohmar, D. (2016). Husserl's Manuscript A I 35. In G. E. Rosado Haddock, ed., *Husserl and Analytic Philosophy*. Berlin: De Gruyter, pp. 289–320.

Maddy, P. (1997). *Naturalism in Mathematics*, Oxford: Oxford University Press.

Maddy, P. (2007). *Second Philosophy: A Naturalistic Method*, Oxford: Oxford University Press.

Maddy, P. (2008). How Applied Mathematics Became Pure. *The Review of Symbolic Logic*, 1 (1), 16–41.

Maddy, P. (2011). *Defending the Axioms: On the Philosophical Foundations of Set Theory*, Oxford: Oxford University Press.

Maddy, P. & Väänänen, J. (2023). *Philosophical Uses of Categoricity Arguments*. Cambridge Elements in the Philosophy of Mathematics. Cambridge: Cambridge University Press.

Mancosu, P. ed. (2008). *Philosophy of Mathematical Practice*, Oxford: Oxford University Press.

Moon, S. (2023). *Husserlian Philosophy of Mathematical Practice: An Empathy-First Approach*. Dissertation. University of California, Irvine.

Okada, M. (2013). Husserl and Hilbert on Completeness and Husserl's Term Rewrite-Based Theory of Multiplicity. 24th International Conference on Rewriting Techniques and Applications, RTA, 4-19.

von Plato, J. (2017). *The Great Formal Machinery Works: Theories of Deduction and Computation at the Origins of the Digital Age*, Princeton: Princeton University Press.

Putnam, H. (1980). Models and Reality. *Journal of Symbolic Logic*, 45 (3), 464–482.

Queloz, M. (2021). *The Practical Origins of Ideas: Genealogy as Conceptual Reverse-Engineering*, Oxford: Oxford University Press.

Rosado Haddock, G. (2006). Husserl's Philosophy of Mathematics: Its Origin and Relevance. *Husserl Studies*, 22, 193–222.

Russell, B. (1903). *Principles of Mathematics*, Cambridge: Cambridge University Press.

Shapiro, S. (1997). *Philosophy of Mathematics, Structure and Ontology*, Oxford: Oxford University Press.

Thomasson, A. (2014). *Ontology Made Easy*, Oxford: Oxford University Press.

Tieszen, R. (2011). *After Gödel: Platonism and Rationalism in Mathematics and Logic*, Oxford: Oxford University Press.

Wachtel, A. (2024). The Phenomenological Concept of Definiteness: Husserl vs. His Interpreters, and Tertium non Datur. *The New Yearbook for Phenomenology and Phenomenological Philosophy*, 22, 188–208.

Weyl, H. (1985). Axiomatic versus Constructive Procedures in Mathematics. *The Mathematical Intelligencer*, 7 (4), 12–17, 38.

Zahavi, D. (2002). Transcendental Subjectivity and Metaphysics: *A Discussion of David Carr's* Paradox of Subjectivity. *Human Studies*, 25, 103–116.

Zahavi, D. (2003). *Husserl's Phenomenology*, Stanford: Stanford University Press.

Zahavi, D. (2017). *Husserl's Legacy: Phenomenology, Metaphysics, and Transcendental Philosophy*, Oxford: Oxford University Press.

Zermelo, E. (1908). Investigations in the Foundations of Set Theory I. In J. van Heijenoort, ed., *From Frege to Gödel: A Source Book in Mathematical Logic, 1879-1931*. Cambridge: Harvard University Press [1967], pp. 201–215.

Zermelo, E. (1930). On Boundary Numbers and Domains of Sets: New Investigations in the Foundations of Set Theory. In W. B. Ewald, ed., *From Kant to Hilbert: A Source Book in the Foundations of Mathematics*, Vol. 2, Oxford: Clarendon Press [1996], pp. 1219–1233.

The Philosophy of Mathematics

Penelope Rush

University of Tasmania

From the time Penny Rush completed her thesis in the philosophy of mathematics (2005), she has worked continuously on themes around the realism/anti-realism divide and the nature of mathematics. Her edited collection, *The Metaphysics of Logic* (Cambridge University Press, 2014), and forthcoming essay 'Metaphysical Optimism' (*Philosophy Supplement*), highlight a particular interest in the idea of reality itself and curiosity and respect as important philosophical methodologies.

Stewart Shapiro

The Ohio State University

Stewart Shapiro is the O'Donnell Professor of Philosophy at The Ohio State University, a Distinguished Visiting Professor at the University of Connecticut, and a Professorial Fellow at the University of Oslo. His major works include *Foundations without Foundationalism* (1991), *Philosophy of Mathematics: Structure and Ontology* (1997), *Vagueness in Context* (2006), and *Varieties of Logic* (2014). He has taught courses in logic, philosophy of mathematics, metaphysics, epistemology, philosophy of religion, Jewish philosophy, social and political philosophy, and medical ethics.

About the Series

This Cambridge Elements series provides an extensive overview of the philosophy of mathematics in its many and varied forms. Distinguished authors will provide an up-to-date summary of the results of current research in their fields and give their own take on what they believe are the most significant debates influencing research, drawing original conclusions.

Cambridge Elements ≡

The Philosophy of Mathematics

Elements in the Series

A full series listing is available at: www.cambridge.org/EPM